COOKING
ON A BOOTSTRAP

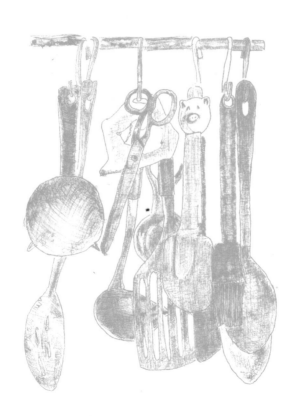

COOKING
ON A BOOTSTRAP

JACK
MONROE

OVER 100 SIMPLE, BUDGET RECIPES

bluebird
books for life

CONTENTS

For Jonathon, my still-Small Boy

INTRODUCTION

Every recipe book I write seems to contain a recipe for lentil soup, and I am unashamed of this. When I was living in my freezing cold flat, scraping together change to buy food to sustain me and my boy through an unforgiving winter, well-meaning friends would advise me to buy a bag of lentils. They're filling, they would say. Cheap, they'd enthuse. A good source of protein, they'd nod enthusiastically. I was sceptical, because the humble lentil was a stranger to me. It was something Other, something unfamiliar, something else. And one of the most poignant things about living on a stringent budget, is you can't afford to experiment with new ideas that may go wrong, or may taste revolting, or may end up burnt and stuck to the pan and inevitably in the bin. There isn't a margin for error and experiment when there isn't a margin for turning on the sodding hallway lights, I would try to explain.

By now, in better times, I have experimented my way through bags of lentils to find well-tested recipes that are simple and sustaining, and, above all, delicious. Dear reader, I am incredibly fussy about what I put in my mouth. It has to bring me joy. It has to satisfy. It has to ignite, to delight, to sing to me. Please, as we go on this journey together, trust me that there is not a single recipe in this book that I do not adore, have not tested and tested and tweaked and improved and sighed over and groaned over and loved and cherished. I write these on postcards, store them in a Jiffy bag marked 'SACRED, HALLOWED, PRECIOUS'.

My mission is simple – that cooking on a budget needn't be gruel and gastronomic flagellation. It can be sumptuous. It can be nourishing. It can be flavourful. It can be devastatingly delicious. It can be restaurant-quality. It can be achievable. It can be all of these things with the smallest of kitchens and the simplest of equipment and absolutely no basic skills whatsoever. It can be yours.

FREQUENTLY ASKED QUESTIONS

As I was writing this book, my wonderful and extraordinarily patient editor, Martha (it takes a whole village to raise a cookery book these days), had the same queries throughout the pile of recipes that I handed her. Is the butter salted or unsalted? Do you weigh your vegetables? They are also the usual questions that I receive online and in letters from my readers, so I thought I would address a few here.

Which rice do you use for risotto?

I use long grain rice over Arborio, as it is, in my humble opinion, just as adequate. Toast it at the edges in a little oil or butter until it becomes translucent, then gradually feed it booze and stock a little at a time, stirring consistently, until soupy and still slightly firm. Some people like their rice al dente, I like mine falling apart in my mouth, but we all like it on a budget and that's why we're here. Arborio rice is admittedly delicious, but I save it for a restaurant wow experience, rather than blow my budget on being pernickety.

Salted or unsalted butter?

I like to choose my own salinity – I think I read that phrase first in *Kitchen* by Nigella Lawson and it resonated with me like a church bell clanging in my culinary heart. A salt fiend, I prefer to add my own, and unfashionably plenty of it.

What can you use instead of butter and olive oil?

In baking, swap butter out for a mild vegetable oil such as sunflower or vegetable, and a tiny pinch of salt. In cooking, do the same, but coconut oil is also a good substitute. Olive oil is always delicious for smearing on toast or some gently cooked veg, but I throw my hands up at the cost of it, so usually revert to rapeseed or sunflower with a good grind of pepper to emulate the darker green oils. The same works when dressing a salad.

I'm vegetarian – what can I substitute in your meat dishes?

My general rule of thumb is that a butter bean is a good hefty substitute for chicken in a soup or casserole, usually with a little carrot in it to sweeten it up. Kidney beans or black beans are a decent swap for beef in a chilli or curry, and cooked long enough they are soft and tender in a way that even the slowest-cooked joints of meat can never quite attain. I sub chorizo with small white beans like haricots or cannellinis, with a hefty dollop of garlic, salt and paprika to imitate the flavour. Don't look at what you can't have, look at what you can. Pack soups out with chickpeas and lentils, sling some veggie sausages in your stews, and find your way around one of my half a dozen veggie burger recipes, and you'll wonder what all the fuss was about anyway.

I don't have that herb …

Herbs shmerbs, although they are all sumptuous little bursts of flavour, they are neither prescriptive nor indispensable, and one can easily be substituted for another if you find you don't have them to hand. As a general rule, I keep rosemary on my window ledge (and a lot of it in my garden, grown from the £1 plant from the supermarket and gently nurtured into a large wild beast). I keep coriander in the freezer, blitzed to a paste with a tiny bit of water and frozen in ice cube trays for ease, and to be honest the rest barely get a look in. I get some mint in the summer, but the slugs like it rather more than I get a chance to, and it keeps them off my hydrangeas, so they're welcome to it. You can swap one wintery herb for another, so flirt between rosemary, thyme, lemon thyme, sage and bay as you fancy. The same with bright herbs; basil, mint, parsley and chives are all fairly interchangeable too.

Smoked bacon or unsmoked?

I always advise people on a low budget to buy packets of 'cooking bacon' (if they are meat eaters, of course), which can be found in the bottom shelves of the supermarket, tucked out of the way. It is a tightly packed wodge of scraps and offcuts, a mixture of smoked and unsmoked, so really, anything goes. Some people prefer the musty taste of smoked bacon, one of my friends says it's like tipping an ashtray into your casserole, so it really is a matter of personal preference.

What size eggs?

For years I bought my eggs in 'mixed weight free range' boxes, as they were cheaper than the uniform half dozen, and have never had a cake fail on me yet. Not a quail's egg, not a goose egg, but anything in between works just fine. We are so sentimental about the science of baking sometimes, but I am here to hurl all of that out of the window and tell you there is no such thing as bad cake. There is cake that sometimes needs to be eaten with ice cream to hold it back together, or cake that needs 5 more minutes in the oven, but they are still both brilliant in their own warm, delicious right.

Granulated sugar?

Again, hurling the cake book out of the window here, but I use white granulated sugar in almost everything. If you have a bullet-style blender and a penchant for absolutes, then just grind it into dust, sieve it, and store it in a jar for baking.

I don't have any red wine for my casserole ...

... then use black tea. It sounds like a mad trick, but it certainly works a treat, imparting the same lip-smacking tannin flavour as a halfway decent bottle of plonk would. Leftover wine can be kept in a jar or bottle beside the oven to add to soups and risottos, and yes, you can sling your table wine in with your dregs of Beaujolais etc etc, in fact I find if I mix them all together in a murk in a jar, I'm less likely to accidentally take a swig when cooking! 'Blended' wine, I call it, rather than 'found behind the couch'.

My soup is too salty . . .

Slice a potato in half and add it to the soup and cook it until done, then lift out the potato. It won't extract all of the salt, but it will certainly help mellow it with an injection of starch. If it is still a little too caustic, add a dash of lemon juice or vinegar to brighten it, and watch the size of your pinches next time!

Plain flour for bread? Really?

Yes. And with over 100 loaves under my rapidly expanding belt, I think I have thoroughly tested this theory enough by now. Plain flour is just as good for baking, thickening sauces, making a roux, a béchamel (white sauce), even making a pasta, pizza base. Again, if you have the money to spend, there are so many wonderful varieties of flour out there to experiment with, but don't let anyone tell you they're essential or turn their nose up at your loaf. All you need is a bag of flour, a bit of yeast, some warm water, and your hands, and you're good to go.

What do I need in my store-cupboard?

Well, turn the page . . .

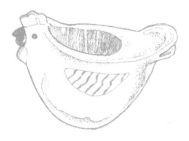

MY KITCHEN STORE-CUPBOARD: A SHOPPING GUIDE

I try to shop with the rules of a healthy balanced diet in mind, although it isn't always easy if you're working to a limited budget. I make my shopping list in four sections. PROTEIN first, as it's generally one of the more expensive food groups. CARBS next, as they're cheap and filling. FRUIT AND VEG from the tinned fruit aisle, the baking department for dried fruit, the freezer department and the fresh produce section. STORE-CUPBOARD for herbs and spices, flavours, and things to generally make your simple ingredients a little more exciting and a lot more versatile.

There's no need to get everything at once – all store-cupboards are built up over time, with a spice picked up here and a vinegar there, a bag of flour one week and a bag of rice or pasta the next. Here are a few essentials that I try to keep kicking around – but please, if you only have a very tiny budget or not much spare, don't feel you have to get everything on this list. Pick a few recipes with similar ingredients to start you off, and go from there.

PROTEIN

Many people associate protein with 'meat', but that doesn't have to be the case. Sources of protein are not just limited to chicken and beef, but can be found in much-cheaper forms. Tins of sardines, for example. Jars of fish paste. Bags of frozen fish fillets. Tins of beans and pulses, or the dried variety to soak and cook in advance. I pack out soups with pulses (kidney beans and chickpeas, usually), and also use tinned beans to make chilli, burgers, curries, daals and stews. Beans, pulses and lentils are easier and cheaper to store than joints of meat, as they can be stashed in a cupboard and have a long shelf life.

DAIRY

A large pot of natural yoghurt goes a long way, either as a standalone breakfast with a little tinned fruit mixed in, or as the base for a smoothie with a fistful of oats, a sauce for meat, a curry base, or to toss through pasta with lemon and herbs. Value-range cheeses are excellent, with Brie, anything hard and strong, and blues all packing a punchy flavour for pennies. The stronger the flavour, the less you need for your recipe, so don't be put off by the whiffier varieties, just use a smaller amount.

CARBS

The cheapest carbohydrates in the shops are invariably, at the time of writing, long grain white rice and tinned potatoes. Brown rice costs more than white rice, despite white rice being processed. Something about supply and demand, I suppose, but I am neither a rice grower nor a supermarket buying controller. The same goes for pasta. White flour, again, is cheaper than wholemeal flour. I go by the principle of 'everything in moderation' – I was brought up on white rice and white bread and I did just fine. Besides, if you are cooking your meals from scratch, from this book, a little white starch isn't going to do you any harm. Especially not as an alternative to salt-and-chemical-laden ready meals, for example. A bag of oats goes a long way, too, for porridge, breakfast smoothies, flapjacks, granola, oat pancakes …

FRUIT

Most supermarkets sell large bags of apples, pears and bananas. They may be small, or wonky, but they're very useful for getting fresh fruit inside you – or your children – for a fraction of the cost of the loose and beautiful ones. Check out the tinned fruits, too. Tinned pineapple, mandarins, peaches and pears are handy to have in the cupboard as a snack, dessert, for flavouring yoghurt or even throwing into a curry. The freezer department is always worth a look, too, for bags of frozen berries much cheaper than their fresh counterparts. I also love a bag of cheap sultanas, for making my own granola, as a snack for my Small Boy, for stirring into porridge, or poshing up a korma, etc.

VEG

I buy most of my vegetables either frozen or tinned, with the exception of large packets of root vegetables. Onions and carrots tend to go in everything, so I buy them by the kilo (at the time of writing this, 1.5kg of Basics carrots are 75p, and 1.5kg Basics onions are 90p). Tinned carrots, tomatoes and sweetcorn are handy store-cupboard staples, and often cheaper than their fresh or frozen counterparts. Tinned peas are cooked for longer, so break down soft and gorgeous in risottos. And mushy peas, if you like that kind of thing, but I am not a fan – although a can of mushy peas with a little stock and cheese makes for instant soup. I buy my greens frozen – spinach, broccoli, peas and green beans are all far cheaper bought frozen, and don't go to waste in the drawer of the fridge.

STORE-CUPBOARD

Dark chocolate can be used as a base for Mexican soups and chillies, melted into cornflakes for quick simple snacks, or for hot chocolate.

Lemon juice Bottled lemon juice is far cheaper than a bag of fresh lemons, and lasts longer. I have used it for years, even serving it up to very 'foodie' friends, and none of them have ever picked up on the difference. I often swap vinegar for lemon juice in recipes where a short sharp shock of acidity is required, too, so don't be afraid to do this as well.

Oil Any oil will do. I use sunflower oil for cooking day to day, for salad dressings and even for baking. Olive oil is nice but useless for roasting as it has a low smoke point, so goes slightly rancid, and is much more expensive. I like the lightness of sunflower oil for making pestos

and marinades and sauces, in that it takes on the flavours of the ingredients it is mixed in, lubricating and emulsifying without taking centrestage.

Raising agents Bicarbonate of soda and yeast are essentials in my store-cupboard as I bake a lot of bread (and cake!) and use them interchangeably in pizza dough. You can make a quick soda bread from just bicarb, lemon juice, flour and milk, so it's useful to keep some to hand.

Spices My essential spices are paprika, cumin and turmeric, and for a long time they were all I had kicking about in my kitchen, with a sad chilli plant struggling on my window ledge. I use them all liberally, to enliven simple ingredients. If you live near an independent grocery store of the ethnic variety, pop your head in, as they usually have large bags of spices far cheaper than the tiny jars in your nearest supermarket.

Stock cubes I generally use chicken stock for everything. There, I said it. But if you are a stock purist, keep a few varieties – most shops do a 'value' range of these too. I use half a stock cube for most recipes with a liberal pinch of salt, meaning they go twice as far.

Wine or beer I buy a bottle of value wine, red or white, and keep it on the side to cook with. Depending on how often I use it, a bottle can last a month. If the thought of spending £3–4 on a botte of wine just to throw into cooking alarms you, you can replace red wine with strong black tea for any slow-cooked recipes, as I mentioned in my Frequently Asked Questions section (see page 8). Several of my readers tried it and couldn't tell the difference. Neither could the friends for whom I made a black tea bourgignon last summer, and most of them worked in restaurants. It's the little tricks ...

KITCHEN EQUIPMENT

You don't need lots of gadgets and fancy whizzy goods in order to knock up good-quality, delicious meals in the smallest of kitchens. I have a lot of kitchen equipment these days, but mostly of the stagnant variety, like wooden spoons, forks, mixing bowls. I dream of a Breville toastie maker, but can't quite justify it when I can just sling a sarnie in the oven pressed between two baking trays for a similar effect. I make ice creams with just a bowl and a whisk, bread with my hands, and until recently, was still rolling out bread dough with an old, clean wine bottle. And you can, too. It helps to have some basics kicking about, but they are just that, basics. If you can't get everything on the list at once, don't panic, just build your little kitchen up as you go. Charity shops are my haven for good-quality kitchen goods; if a quirky little baking dish has survived since the 1970s to turn up in your local Oxfam, chances are it's going to last you a lifetime. I found a spotless Le Creuset saucepan in my local Mind store last year for £3 and ran home with it as though I had stolen it. Quaint old, beautiful cutlery goes for pennies. My Mason Cash mixing bowl, large enough to mix a kilo of bread in, was £1. Crystal decanters and mismatched glassware from years gone by can be picked up for small change, gosh, the decadence. I may not have had much to live on in my worst days, but I could drink my tap water from a 20p Royal Doulton glass.

Pans 1 large-as-you-dare saucepan, for what holds a lot will hold a little. 1 smaller saucepan for sauces and one-person meals and reheating cold coffee. 1 large frying pan or sauté pan, preferably with a lid but you can always fashion one out of tin foil or a large plate, or a large plate covered in tin foil.

In the oven 1 deep roasting tin, for deeply roasting things. 1 baking sheet for pizzas, cookies, bread, etc. 1 loaf tin if you care about your loaves being loaf shaped. 1 muffin tin because everyone likes muffins.

In the drawer 2 wooden spoons. A good masher, the wavy kind is easier to clean but the L-shaped holey kind is super satisfying if you have a lot of rage to get out by dinner time. General cutlery. A small sharp knife. A large sharp knife. A knife sharpener to keep those knives sharp, or if you really won't, get serrated ones and be done with it. Kitchen scissors are also handy, a vegetable peeler, and a grater.

On the worktop A small blender. I have a Bullet-style blender these days as it gets a fair bit of use and the basic jug blenders were blowing up on a monthly basis during the testing phase of this book! It was around £20 from a well-known hardware and home store, and easily competes with its expensive rivals. A tin opener.

Scales I only really use scales for bread or cake recipes, as everything else is done by handfuls and pinches and whatever's kicking around in the fridge, but they are handy to have. Again, charity shops are your friend here, bul basic small kitchen scales are only a couple of pounds.

A large mixing bowl or two I get most of mine from the pound shop, and they've lasted for three cookbooks and a good few years now. A little dented, but they polish up lovely.

And that's it. If you want to make life easier, you can get tongs for turning burgers and other things, a julienne peeler for shredding veg into pickles and salads and slaw and that trendy vegetable-as-pasta thing, and a few extra knives and spoons.

BREAD

Having a basic bread recipe up your sleeve is a life-changing thing; the ability to rustle up a fresh warm loaf with nothing more than a 50p bag of flour and a few store-cupboard ingredients is an art form, but one that is very simple to learn. The rise of the modern 'breadmaker' appliance almost instilled a fear in me that making bread was for other people, or so impossibly difficult that it needed this new-fangled machine in order to help me navigate its complexities, and so I put it off for years, believing that I couldn't do it. Lo and behold, when I first turned my hand to making bread, I laughed at how simple it really was. And it is. Years later, I have not bought a loaf of bread nor a roll for as long as I can remember. I have a large bread bin in my hallway (my kitchen is so small that the hallway has become a sort-of larder of bookshelves stuffed with kitchen equipment), and it is filled with different kinds of flour. As my Small Boy knows, if we want bread, in our house, we make it ourselves.

BASIC WHITE (VE)

MAKES 1 SMALL LOAF

400g plain flour, plus extra for dusting

1 tsp sugar (optional)

a pinch or two of salt

6–7g dried active yeast (1.5 level tsp)

250ml warm water

1 tsp oil

We begin with a loaf of basic white bread, in measurements suitable for a household of one hungry person or one adult and a small child. I have deliberately made the measurements easy to adjust with no compromise on taste, but would rarely bake a loaf with more than 600g flour as a base because bread is best when it is fresh, and I would rather split a larger batch of dough in two, bake them both together, and freeze one loaf for later use.

Even though this dough can be quickly thrown together in the evening or morning and left to rise in the fridge for no longer than 24 hours, then baked later, working hours mean that I don't always have the time to do this daily. So I often triple or even quadruple this recipe and split the dough into rolls and a loaf, then freeze anything that will not be used in the next two days. This maximises the use of the oven to save on energy costs, and it also means you don't have to bake every day.

There is much kerfuffle about the use of white flour among the new wave of elitist health-foodies. I say pish and tosh. If you are making your own food from scratch with no chemicals or preservatives or other added oddities, a little white flour isn't going to kill you. There are healthier recipes further along in this chapter, but please, white bread is joyous, delicious, and it is also a third of the price of its pious counterparts. Enjoy it.

1 Measure the flour into a large mixing bowl and add the remaining dry ingredients: the sugar (if using), salt and yeast. Mix well but briefly.

2 Make a well in the centre (a sort of hole) and add most of the warm water. Stir well to combine, bringing the dry ingredients from the edges of the bowl into the centre and mixing to form a dough. If the dough looks dry and is cracking, add the remaining water. If it is tacky and sticking to your fingers, add a shake more flour.

3 Lightly flour the work surface. Tip the dough onto it, scraping any stubborn bits from the edges of the bowl. Oil your hands and start to knead the dough. You can knead for 2–3 minutes if your wrists are weak or you tire easily, but 10 is recommended. Don't knead for longer than that, though, or the dough will tighten up and fail to rise adequately in the oven. If it does become stiff and unworkable, simply pop it in a bowl, cover it with cling film or a clean tea towel and leave it at room temperature for half an hour, to allow it to relax again and breathe. Leave it to rise for an hour, at room temperature, or until doubled in size.

4 Preheat the oven to 180°C/350°F/gas 4. Lightly flour a baking sheet. Tip the risen dough onto the baking sheet and lightly shape it with your hands into a round. Loaf tins are overrated – I love a freeform round crusty loaf. Take a sharp knife and score an X in the middle of the top of the loaf. Dust with flour.

5 Pop the baking sheet on the middle shelf of the oven and bake for 40 minutes. When it's cooked, it should sound hollow when tapped on the bottom. If it feels slightly dense, or a sharp knife inserted in the middle comes out a little sticky, pop it back in the oven for another 10 minutes. When cooked, remove it from the oven and transfer the bread to a wire rack to cool.

TIP

● If you are really befuddled about kneading dough, there are some great videos online – type in 'how to knead dough' on a search engine and thousands of demonstrations come up.

SIMPLE FLATBREADS (V)

1 cup (235ml) milk

1 tsp sugar

1 tsp dried active yeast

3 cups (375g) plain flour (bread flour if you're feeling fancy, but it really isn't necessary), plus extra for dusting

1 tsp oil

a pinch of salt

Flatbreads are incredibly easy to knock up with the most meagre of ingredients, and once made, they can be frozen until needed, then warmed through, dunked in soup, dips, oil, eaten as a snack, fashioned into makeshift pizzas, or used as a vehicle for leftovers for lunch the next day.

These take around half an hour from start to finish – faster than your average bread recipe – and need no more specialist equipment than your own bare hands, a bowl and a baking tray. I have dispensed with traditional measurements for this recipe as I never bother to weigh it – pick a small vessel, a cup of your choice, and work from there, or you can measure out, if you prefer. The milk can be replaced with water or any dairy-free milk substitute that you may normally use. I have made these with coconut milk, too, having half a tin kicking about from some curry or another, and it was utterly delicious. Use this as a guide, and go as wild as your cupboards and your budget will let you.

Makes as many as it makes, depending on size of cup and size of breads. Easily multipliable for larger batches.

1 First heat the milk very gently in a small pan, or in a mug in the microwave, until warm to the touch. You don't want it hot, or it will kill the yeast, and you're relying on that to make your flatbreads. When warm (dipping a tentative finger should elicit an ahhhh, not an arrrrghhhh), remove from the heat and add the sugar and yeast. Mix well and stand it to one side.

2 Grab a large mixing bowl and tip the flour into it, through a sieve if you have one, but don't worry if not. These things are often thought essential but I did without them for many years and still turned out perfectly good breads and things. Now that I own a sieve, I use it when I remember – for cakes I am desperate to impress people with or anything that requires a lighter touch – but mostly I consider it a faff. Simple cooking is simple cooking, after all, and a pile of washing up is a ghastly business when there is life to be lived instead.

COOKING ON A BOOTSTRAP

3 Make a well in the centre of the flour – that is, a rough wide hole. Pour the milky yeasty mixture into it, and the oil, and add the salt, then mix well to form a dough. If it is too dry and crumbly, add a splash more milk. If it is too sloppy, add some more flour, and so on. When it is doughy, gently flour the worktop, and tip it out.

4 Knead the dough for a few minutes, pushing it out with your knuckles to stretch it, folding it back in half, turning it over, and repeating. After a few minutes you should feel it become fairly uniform and springy to touch, as it quite literally comes alive under your hands. Breadmaking always fascinates me, and this part of the process is my favourite, the physical creation of something good from so little, something responsive, nourishing and comforting.

5 With a sharp knife, cut the dough into equal-sized pieces, depending on the size or number of breads you want to make. Though they be little, they be but filling (to bastardise the Bard somewhat!). Lightly flour a baking tray and pop on the breads. Cover with a tea towel and leave in a warm place for 20 minutes at room temperature to rise. I have been known to put them on a plate and sling them in the microwave on the defrost setting for a couple of minutes to kickstart this process, a theory that elicits impressed nods from some baking friends and pearl-clutching shrieks from others. Up to you if you want to risk it, but it can save a bit of time if you are in a hurry. Don't be tempted to ping it on a higher heat, though, as you will just make it crusty and forlorn and have to start again. Take it from a fool who tried, so you don't have to.

6 As they rise, preheat the oven to 200°C/400°F/gas 6. If they are reluctant to grow, pop the tray in the warming oven for a minute to warm them through – that should get them going.

7 When risen, gently roll them out to around 3mm thick. Place them back on the baking tray and cook for around 8 minutes, or until risen and golden. Remove from the tray onto a wire rack and allow to cool slightly before serving.

8 For extra pizzazz, if you have a gas hob, light the biggest one and sling the flatbreads onto it, one by one, for 10 seconds at a time to char the edges – if you like that kind of thing. I do it for mine, but not the Boy Child, as he just complains his bread is burnt. It's not burnt, son, it's authentic. Honest.

APPLESAUCE BREADCAKE (VE)

SERVES 8, CUT INTO
CHUNKY SQUARES
OR SLICES

**2 small dessert
apples, any kind
will do**

**1 tbsp bottled lemon
juice**

**100ml oil, plus extra
for greasing**

225g plain flour

**1½ level tsp
bicarbonate of soda**

**1 tsp ground
cinnamon, or more
or less, depending
on taste**

**a generous handful
of sultanas or mixed
dried peel (optional)**

This applesauce bread-that's-a-bit-cakey is based on my original vegan banana bread recipe from my first cookbook, *A Girl Called Jack*. Photographs of that banana bread are sent to me on a near-daily basis, with an especial flurry at weekends, and I am delighted to receive them. It remains one of my favourite recipes, but every now and again a reader gets in touch to say that they just really don't like bananas. At all. It seemed a shame not to share the simplicity and deliciousness of one of my favourite recipes with bananaphobes, so, I set about creating one just as simple, with Something Else.

The Something Else turned out to be apple sauce, made from stewing apples – this can be cheated in the microwave for an even simpler version, or use a jar of shop-bought apple sauce.

As this is a yeast-free and quite dense bread, it will work well with gluten-free flour – simply add a splash of water, and then another towards the end, and mix in well to form the dough. Gluten-free flour tends to need more liquid than its regular counterparts.

1 **First dice the apples. I leave the skin on mine with a quick wash under the tap, as there is fibre in the skin and a lot of the vitamins reportedly sit just beneath. You won't notice it anyway, as it will be mushed down and baked into a loaf! Toss them into a pan with the lemon juice to stop them browning. Cover with water, bring to a boil, and reduce to a simmer for around 20 minutes or until softened.**

2 **Preheat the oven to 180°C/350°F/gas 4 and lightly grease a 900g/2lb loaf tin. (If you don't have a loaf tin, a cake tin will do, or even mound it on a baking tray.)**

Recipe continues overleaf

3 Take a large mixing bowl and add the flour, bicarbonate of soda and cinnamon. I have deliberately not put sugar in this recipe as I find the small cheap apples sweet enough, but if you are using a cooking apple or a more tart variety, you might want to add 2 tablespoons of caster sugar to the mix. Stir it all together to evenly distribute.

4 Drain any excess water from the cooked apples, but reserve the liquid in case you need it later – not all dough is created equal and this water will be apple-flavoured! Add the apples to a bowl and mash them with a fork, adding the oil gradually to create a loose applesauce mixture.

5 Make a well (a sort of hole) in the centre of the dry ingredients, and pour in the applesauce and sultanas or dried peel. Mix well to form a thick batter, adding a splash of the reserved apple-water if necessary. It should be reasonably stiff to stir but not dry and cracking.

6 Dollop the dough into your vessel of choice – loaf tin, cake tin or on a baking tray. If using a baking tray, flour your hands well and roughly shape your batter to hold it together somewhat. Err on the side of tall and round as it may spread as well as rise.

7 Pop it into the oven and bake for 40 minutes, or until a sharp knife or skewer inserted into the middle comes out clean. Transfer to a wire rack to cool before slicing. Store in an airtight bag or container and keep for up to 3 days, or in the freezer for up to 3 months.

COOKING ON A BOOTSTRAP

SPROUT SCONES (V)

MAKES 6 AVERAGE-
SIZED SCONES OR
4 LARGE ONES

**80g Brussels sprouts
or a generous
handful of leafy
greens, finely sliced**

**200g self-raising
flour**

**1 level tsp
bicarbonate of soda**

a pinch of salt

50ml milk (any kind)

**2 medium or large
eggs**

**40g cheese, of any
variety (optional)**

**a splash of oil,
for frying**

Sniff not, leftovers fans, for this is a delicious and delightful way to use up any leftover greens hanging around from recent festive dinners. Spring greens work just as well, and spinach, or a combination of anything green and leafy, really. Knobbly, straggly ends and rinds of cheese can be incorporated into these, too, for a baked brunch or lunchtime treat that is so much more than the sum of its parts.

This recipe can be made vegan by using a plant milk of your choosing, and swapping the eggs for 4 tablespoons of aquafaba (the water that sits in a tin of chickpeas!) and, of course, using vegan cheese. Serve warm and buttered with a topping of your choice. (Pictured overleaf.)

1 Toss the sprouts or greens into a mixing bowl. Add the flour, the bicarb and salt and make a well (a kind of hole) in the centre of the dry ingredients. Pour the milk into the well, and crack the eggs on top. Crumble in your cheese here, if using any.

2 Mix well with a wooden spoon until it comes together into a pliable, but not too sticky, dough. If it sticks unpleasantly to your hands, add a tablespoon of flour. If it cracks, add a splash of water. Dough is rarely unresolvable, especially at this stage, once you have a few tricks up your sleeve. So if you're unfamiliar with dough, don't panic; just tinker a bit until you have something you can roll around in your hand without leaving too much of it stuck to your fingers!

3 Flour your work surface and tip the dough onto it. Knead briefly – working the dough with your knuckles and palms to stretch it a little – but not for long, as it isn't a yeast-based dough, so barely needs any handling. It's more to give it an even consistency, the same way as you might warm up Play-Doh or plasticine before using it, rather than the more complex and enduring method of kneading bread dough. Roll it out with a rolling pin or flatten it with your hands to around 2cm thick. Using a cookie cutter, or the top of a glass and a knife, cut scones from the dough to your preferred size.

4 Heat a little oil in a frying pan over medium heat and drop in each round of dough – you may need to cook them in batches. Fry for a few minutes on each side, or until risen and golden. Keep the scones warm while you cook the others until you run out of dough! Serve warm.

UNFUCKUPABLE WHOLEMEAL PIZZA DOUGH (VE)

120g wholemeal flour

**120g plain flour, plus
extra for dusting**

**5g dried active yeast
(a heaped teaspoon)**

½ tsp salt (optional)

**1 tbsp oil, plus extra
for greasing**

**200–220ml warm
water, depending
on flour (not all
wholemeals are
created equal)**

I find a good homemade dough recipe makes all the difference to not feeling guilty about indulging in a pizza, but if like me you don't have wholemeal flour in the house all that often, just use all plain flour and sod it. I just included the wholemeal here as a nod to something healthy, but kudos to you for making your own dough anyway!

1 First pop the flours in a mixing bowl and add the yeast and salt, if using. Mix well to combine. Some people like to sift their flour and other dry ingredients together; go ahead by all means if you have a sieve and like to do things properly, but I've never noticed the difference. I am a Neanderthal in some respects, though, and the subtle nuances of a crumb structure often evade me as I ram a pizza into my gob, so such delicate additional steps are wasted on me.

2 Make a well (a sort of hole) in the middle of the dry ingredients and add the oil, followed by most of the warm water. Make sure the water isn't too hot, or else it will kill the yeast – it is a living organism and doesn't take too kindly to being boiled alive!

3 Mix well from the soggy centre outwards, to form a supple dough. I use the handle of a fork or spoon for mixing bread these days, as it stops the dough from gathering in the bowl of the spoon. Grab a wooden spoon and lube it up with cooking oil a few centimetres from the end and up (I demonstrated this to someone once and was met with open-mouthed horror, safe to say if I ever do accept any of those telly offers, I won't be practically demonstrating this one). ANYWAY, use this to stir your dough and it will form fast and smooth and shouldn't stick too much. The usual dough rules apply; if it's too wet and tacky, add a handful of flour. If it's too dry and cracking, add a splash more water.

4 Flour the worktop, and while you're at it, lightly dust the baking tray, too. Tip out the dough, leaving the mixing bowl to one side because you'll need it in a moment. Knead well for a few minutes – you'll feel it becoming soft and supple and springy in your hands. I like to oil my palms to knead, it stops them getting crusty and makes for a rather enjoyable experience.

It's essentially pushing the dough out with your palm, folding it in half, turning it a little, and repeating. There are many ways up the mountain, you just need to stretch it out and work it a little, to activate the gluten. Oily hands seem to keep it all warm, which is another reason why I do it.

5 When you have kneaded the dough, pop it back in the mixing bowl and cover it with cling film or a clean tea towel. Leave in a warm place for 90 minutes, or if the room is a little cool, 2 hours. If your home is bloody cold, like mine is, wrap the covered bowl in two thick bath towels or fleecy blankets/jumpers/a dressing gown to insulate it. It works. Don't clean the flour off your worktop, you'll need it again in a bit. Unless it's really going to bother you, in which case, go right ahead.

6 Preheat the oven to 180°C/350°F/gas 4. Tip out the risen dough onto the floury worktop and roll it out – if you don't have a rolling pin, a wine bottle works just fine. Carefully lift the dough and drop it onto your floured baking tray. Top with desired toppings and leave to prove for 15 minutes to get one last rise out of it – then cook for 15–18 minutes in the centre of the oven, depending on how much you loaded the top!

SOCCA GLUTEN-FREE FRYING-PAN PIZZA BASE (VE)

SERVES 2

120g gram flour

1 tbsp mixed dried herbs

a pinch of salt

4 tbsp oil

When I was indulging in one of my 'health binges', I bought a bag of gram flour from the supermarket. It's not as cheap as Basics flour, but it is gluten-free and very versatile, or so I'm told. I used to shuffle past it in the supermarket, eyeballing it, wondering what could be done with it other than bind my bhaji, so to speak.

And then I took the plunge. And brought it home. I have used it as the binder and coating on my new kidney bean and peanut butter burgers, for an extra smidge of protein, and just to get the bag open and into my consciousness. And I have ended up here. I picked some chard from the garden, and in my house the larger leaves of chard end up on pizzas – a compromise for kids: you can have pizza for dinner sure, but I'm going to cover it in greens.

1 In a large mixing bowl, whisk the gram flour, herbs and salt with 2 tablespoons of oil and gradually add 250ml water to form a very runny batter. I'll admit I was eyeing it suspiciously thinking I had done it wrong, but I was working with four different socca recipes on my table and hadn't deviated wildly from any of them, so that quieted the suspicious little voice.

2 Leave it to one side at room temperature for at least half an hour (1 hour would be better) for the mixture to settle and thicken slightly.

3 Heat a good non-stick frying pan either in the oven at 180°C/350°F/gas 4 or on high heat on the hob until it's hot hot hot. Remove from the heat and add the remaining 2 tablespoons of oil to the pan, then pour in the batter. Cook on high heat for a few minutes until the base is starting to crisp, then reduce the heat to medium and cook for a further 10 minutes, either in the oven or on the hob. The hob will give a crisper base whereas the oven will cook it more evenly all the way through. Remove from the heat when the edges start to come away from the side of the pan.

4 Now top it! I like to smear 2 tablespoons of tomato purée on mine, a fistful of chard and some dollops of Basics cream cheese – but everyone's perfect pizza is a different beast, which is why I only give the base as the recipe!

FIVE-MINUTE BREAD (VE)

MAKES 4
FLATBREADS

**100g self-raising
flour, plus extra for
dusting**

**⅓ tsp bicarbonate of
soda**

a pinch of salt

**70ml soya milk
(or any other milk
equivalent)**

**½ tsp lemon juice or
vinegar**

One September morning, while he was off school and recovering from surgery, my Small Boy announced he wanted 'dippy bread' for breakfast. Bread with something to dip it into, I surmised. Seems fair enough – who doesn't enjoy dunking warm bread into something soft and viscous, and ramming it in their gob? I made a yoghurt dip and whipped last night's leftover roasted squash with a little coconut milk, then realised we didn't have any bread. Drat. He was struggling to walk, so I was reluctant to drag him up the steep hill to the nearest shop, and at seven he was just slightly too small to be left alone while I bravely hunted down our breakfast, so I decided to make some bread. Instant bread, because as the parent of any hungry child knows, there are nanoseconds between being a bit hungry and full-scale tantrum hungry. I set a 5-minute timer, just to see, but I'm an avid baker, so give yourself eight to start with and see how quickly you can break your own record.

1 Preheat the oven to 220°C/425°F/gas 7, you'll need this in just a minute! Pop a large non-stick frying pan onto the hob but don't heat it yet.

2 Grab a large mixing bowl and pour in the flour. Add the bicarb and salt and give it a quick but thorough stir. Pour in the milk and lemon juice and mix vigorously for a minute to form a dough.

3 Tip the dough onto a lightly floured work surface and briefly knead it to bring it together, just for a minute. Divide the dough evenly into four pieces and roll each into a ball. Now turn on the heat under the frying pan to high.

4 Roll each ball out with a rolling pin until about 4mm thick, then pop them into the hot frying pan, two at a time. Cook on high heat for 1 minute, then flip them over for 30 seconds. Transfer them to the oven to keep warm and finish off cooking, then fry the other two.

5 And you're done. Now you can go into your day knowing that you're only ever 3 minutes away from freshly baked bread. Now if you'll excuse me, I'm a tad competitive, so I'm just setting myself a 4-minute timer over here …

COCONUT MILK SODA BREAD (VE)

250g plain flour, plus extra for dusting

1 level tsp bicarbonate of soda

2 tsp lemon juice, fresh or bottled

180ml coconut milk, from a tin (pop the rest in a different container in the fridge to use in the next three days, but it cannot be stored in the tin)

Sometimes I think I want another baby, and so I go to bake some bread while I mull it over. A 40-minute incubation period later, and I'm rocking a warm snuggly bundle against my hip that will sleep all night, not chew my nipple or eject sour milk down my back, and you know, I'm over it. This is one of those recipes for one of those days, and based on my original easy-peasy soda bread, but suitable for vegans and lactose-intolerant folk, too. If you want to use cow's milk instead, as coconut can be a little pricey, feel free. This is a small loaf, but the recipe can be doubled or tripled for larger homes – just turn the oven down to 160°C/325°F/gas 3 after the first half an hour and add an extra 30 minutes of cooking at the end.

1 Preheat the oven to 180°C/350°F/gas 4 and dust a baking tray with flour.

2 Mix the flour and bicarb together in a large mixing bowl until evenly distributed. Soda bread doesn't take much kneading, so it's better to evenly scatter the bicarb throughout when mixing than end up with a wonky loaf.

3 Squeeze or pour the lemon juice into the coconut milk, depending on whether you are using a fresh lemon or the bottled stuff – I have never noticed a difference between the two in cooking and always keep a bottle kicking around.

4 Make a well (a kind of hole) in the middle of the dry ingredients and pour in the milk and lemon juice mixture. Mix firmly but briefly until just combined, then tip out the dough onto a floured worktop. Knead for 30 seconds, no more, just to bring it together. Pat it into shape and pop it on the baking tray.

5 Score the loaf down the middle – that is, cut it lightly with a sharp knife, then dust the top with flour from your work surface. Bake for 40 minutes. Allow to cool slightly on the tray, then slice and enjoy. Store in an airtight bag or container and keep for up to 3 days, or in the freezer for up to 3 months.

PINT-GLASS BREAD (VE)

2 pint glasses of plain flour, plus extra for dusting

1 pint glass of warm beer

1 tsp dried active yeast

a pinch of salt

1 tsp sugar

oil, for the dough and greasing

This is the easiest and tastiest bread, from only five ingredients. You will need: a bag of flour (mine is a supermarket basic, but any flour will do), some dried active yeast granules and some beer. Salt and sugar are useful if you have them in the house, and we will be using negligible amounts of them, so please, no hands thrown up in horror or faux-pearl-clutching here – my rule is you can eat all the junk you want as long as you make it yourself. A little oil is helpful when making bread, for a smoother dough and a crispy crust, and any oil works. I make this bread with supermarket value-range bitter but it also works with cider. Grab a mixing bowl and wooden spoon and follow me.

1 Stand your pint glass in a large mixing bowl, then fill it with flour. Tip it into the bowl and repeat. Use the butt, or bottom, or arse, of your glass to make a well in the flour.

2 Pour half the beer into the pint glass and ping it in the microwave for 40 seconds or thereabouts to warm it through. Warming it helps wake up your little yeast granules from their slumber, so your bread can rise and shine. Top up with the rest of the beer – too hot and the yeast will die. You want it to be pleasantly warm, not scalding.

3 Pour the beer into the middle of the flour. Add the yeast, salt, sugar and a dash of oil and mix well to make a dough. (I oil the handle of my wooden spoon and use it to stir the mixture, like a dough hook but not attached to a fancypants mixer, attached to me instead.) Mix briskly until the dough comes together – if it is cracking hugely, add a small amount of water. If it's tacky, add a shake of flour.

4 Flour your work surface generously, then tip the dough onto it and start to knead it. Kneading is one of those things that sounded complicated and terrifying when I read about it in books – if someone had just said to me 'punch the crap out of it and make sure you fold it and turn it around every now and then' I would have made bread far earlier. This is the therapy part. Drive your knuckles into the dough to stretch it away from you. Fold it over from the back to the front. Turn it around a bit. Repeat. There's no real wrong way to do it, just work out what feels right for you.

Recipe continues overleaf

5 Oil your hands, go on, lube them up. It feels nice, and it's good for your dough, too. Knead for 5–10 minutes, depending on how angry you are, how patient you are, how much strength you have in your hands and arms, or how many children or dogs are sitting at your feet demanding your love and looking askance at the beige thing you are petting on the worktop.

6 Pop it back into the bowl and cover it with cling film, if you have it, or a clean tea towel. Pop the bowl somewhere warm and leave it for an hour, or overnight for a tangy bread that's a bit like a sourdough and really rather lovely – the beer and yeast ferment, and it's delicious.

7 Preheat the oven to 180°C/350°F/gas 4. Dust the work surface with flour, or, if you're like me, you didn't clean it from the first time round and it's still good to go. Tip out the dough onto the work surface. Roughly mould the dough to your preferred shape – mine is a bit long and chubby. Take a knife and score three slashes into it about a centimetre or so deep – Irish folklore says that this is to let the fairies out, and I like that.

8 Dust the top with some of the worktop flour, and stick the bread straight onto the middle shelf of the oven for 1 hour. You don't need to put it on a baking tray – if you're worried about flour on the bottom of your oven, you can put it on a tray, or for ultimate lazy points, before you turn the oven on line the bottom with a sheet of kitchen roll, and throw it out when it's gross. I like to spend some of that hour tidying the kitchen, although to be fair here we have a spoon, a bowl and a ledge to tidy up, and our hands, too. I kind of aim for minimum equipment and washing up with my recipes because I am lazy, and I live by myself – unless you count the Small Boy, and he is even worse at dishes than I am.

9 When the hour is up, open the oven door, grab a tea towel or oven gloves (I don't have oven gloves but my mum does and so do some other people), and remove your bread. Look at it in awe and wonder. Inhale its brilliant bread smell. Turn it over and tap its bum – if it sounds hollow, it's done. If you're unsure, insert a sharp knife in the middle and see if it comes out clean, but anyway, if it's a bit raw by the time you get to the middle part, just toast it to cook it.

10 Leave it to cool for 10 minutes on a wire rack, then slice it and enjoy. I don't have a bread knife either, so I just use a large normal knife and tear it with my hands. I'm feral, and unapologetic. So there you have it. Pint-glass bread.

CORN MUFFINS (V)

50g softened butter, diced, or 50ml oil (if you're totally brassic), plus extra for greasing

250g plain flour, plus extra for dusting

½ tsp salt

2 tsp baking powder

50g granulated sugar

¼ tsp chilli flakes or 2 pinches of cayenne pepper

70g tinned or frozen sweetcorn, drained

½ small onion, very finely chopped

handful of fresh parsley or coriander, very finely chopped

1 medium egg

250ml milk

Not quite cornbread in the traditional sense, these joyous little bursts of bready sweetness are ideal for mopping up a chilli, topping with an egg and some greens for a speedy brunch, or packing in a picnic or lunchbox. I like to double the batch and pop some in the freezer for a lazy day.

1 Preheat the oven to 200°C/400°F/gas 6, then lightly grease your baking receptacle of choice (be it a deep muffin tin, a 450g/1lb loaf tin or a 20cm shallow round cake tin – any will do but baking times will vary depending on what you are cooking in) to stop your delicious soon-to-be-cornbread from sticking to it.

2 Add the flour, salt, baking powder and sugar to a large mixing bowl with the chilli flakes or a pinch or two of cayenne and give it a stir. Mash the sweetcorn in a bowl roughly with a fork then fold through the muffin mixture – you can roughly blitz it in a blender for a smoother consistency if you like, it depends on your feelings towards 'texture' in your loaves (and if you have fussy children, teenagers or even grown-ups in your house who will eye easily-identifiable vegetables in bread with suspicion and realise it's not the 'cake' you might have told them it was). Add the onion and parsley or coriander to the muffin mix; if you're blitzing the corn in a blender or food processor, feel free to fling these in too for an easy life.

3 Make a well (a sort of hole) in the centre of the mixing bowl and crack in the egg, then pour in most of the milk and beat in the butter or oil to form a soft and slightly sticky dough – it should be looser than a normal bread dough but a lot thicker than a batter – if it struggles to fall off your spoon, you're doing it right. If it's too runny, add an extra tablespoon of flour. If it's too stiff, add a splash more milk or a little water to loosen it.

4 Pour the batter into the tin you're baking in and sprinkle the top with flour. If making a loaf, score a split down the centre – in Soda Bread Theory, this is to let the fairies out, and I like the thought of fairies baking my bread, so I always do this. If making muffins, make a small X in the top of each one. Place in the centre of the oven – a loaf will need 40 minutes to cook, the muffins around 18, but check after 15 minutes and insert a sharp knife into the centre to check that they are cooked through – it should come out clean with no sticky bits on it.

5 Take out of the oven and allow to cool for 10 minutes before removing from the tin. The bread will need a further 10 minutes cooling to firm up before slicing, whereas the muffins are ready to eat almost immediately, if you have an asbestos tongue, that is . . . I like to dip mine warm into softened butter, or halve them and fill them with grated cheese while still warm and let it melt and stick together in the middle. The muffins will keep for 3 days in an airtight container. If I make the loaf, I slice it and freeze it in slices, ready to be toasted or defrosted at will. The muffins freeze well, too.

LARDY BUNS (V)

MAKES 6
GENEROUSLY
WEIGHTY ONES,
WHICH COULD
PROBABLY
SERIOUSLY INJURE
AN ASSAILANT IF
REQUIRED

**1 tsp fast-action
dried yeast**

150ml warm water

**250g plain flour, plus
extra for dusting**

½ tsp salt

**1 tsp ground
cinnamon**

**100g sultanas or
chopped dried fruit
of your choice**

**50g softened butter,
plus extra for
greasing**

100g softened lard

**1 medium egg,
for basting (not
essential)**

50g granulated sugar

I'll always remember my first ever lardy cake, picked up from a surprisingly well-stocked petrol station on the way home from Kent. I slept all the way back in the passenger seat, snoring softly, satiated by soft, sweet carbohydrates and claggy, fatty goodness. When I awoke, the taste of orange peel and grease still on my lips, I flipped the packet over and scrawled down the list of ingredients, then set about making my own. My late, great Greek Cypriot grandfather always cooked in lard, and, seeking to emulate him in every way (he is also responsible for my boilersuit fetish and potty mouth), I also kept a block of it in my kitchen every now and then. If the idea of lard horrifies you, you can use coconut oil, which can be bought in the World Foods aisle at the supermarket far more cheaply than the fancypants raw, organic versions in health-food stores. Not one for every day of the week, but a good shoulders-down, satisfying, occasional comfort, especially toasted, especially on picnics, and especially with a good cup of tea.

1 Kickstart the yeast – spoon it into a mug and add 50ml of the comfortably warm water – remember yeast is a living organism, so if it's too hot for you it's too hot for your yeast! Early on in my breadmaking days I made the mistake of using near-boiling water, foolishly thinking that the hotter it was the better rise I would get on my bread. My bread still rose, and was yummy, but these days it's lighter and yummier with happier yeast. We live and learn. Set it to one side for a moment to start to bubble and grow – trust me, your bread will be better for it.

2 Tip the flour into a large mixing bowl (some people like to sift it to get more air into it, I'm not fussy) and add the salt, cinnamon and dried fruit. Mix well to evenly distribute the ingredients.

3 Make a well (a sort of hole) in the centre of the dry ingredients, and pour in the yeast mixture. Mix well, adding the butter, lard, and the rest of the warm water gradually to form a soft dough. You might not need all of the water – it should be soft and pliable but not tacky. If it's too dry and crumbly, add a

splash more water. If it sticks to your fingers, add a tablespoon or two more flour. It's rarely an exact science – all flours are not created equal – and I'm not in favour of prescriptive recipes anyway.

4 Lightly flour the work surface and your hands, and tip the dough onto it. Knead it, using your knuckles and the heel of your palm to stretch it out, folding it over, turning it, and repeating, until it is soft and springy. There isn't an exact time for this procedure – it depends on your patience levels, experience, strength, speed and technique, but basically your dough should be easy to work with and springy to touch. If it stiffens up, it usually means the gluten has overworked itself, so just cover the bowl with cling film or a clean tea towel and rest it for half an hour in a warm place to let it loosen up before giving it a quick knead again.

5 When it's ready, pop the dough back into the bowl, cover with a clean tea towel or cling film, and leave in a warm place for 1 hour or until doubled in size.

6 Preheat the oven to 180°C/350°F/gas 4 and lightly grease a baking tray. Add a bit more flour to the work surface, tip out the dough and roll it out to around 1cm thick. Using a sharp knife, cut it into strips around 3cm wide. Roll each up into a spiral, tucking the end under the bottom to tidy it up, then brush the top and sides with a little beaten egg, if you like. Pop the spiral buns onto the baking tray and sprinkle lightly with the sugar. Bake for 30 minutes, or until risen and golden. Remove from the oven and cool a little on a warm rack to serve warm, or leave until they are cold and eat them plain or with – heaven forfend – a little more butter spread over them.

CAKEY-GOODNESS BREAD (VE)

100g salted peanuts

200g plain flour, plus extra for dusting

200g wholemeal flour

1 tsp dried active yeast

a pinch of salt

1 tbsp oil

300ml warm water

My boy loves this bread spread thickly with honey, hence the title Cakey-goodness Bread (although that means it is no longer vegan, obviously). One day I might tell him it's more of a wholemeal bread than an actual cake, but until then, I'm enjoying cramming him with unbeknown goodness. Good for grown-ups, too – I like mine with butter and Marmite and strong cheese, and sometimes with marmalade …

1 First soak the peanuts in a bowl of cold water for 30 minutes. Drain and rinse them thoroughly to remove any excess salt, then shake them in a clean tea towel or kitchen roll to dry them. If you want to speed up the process and don't mind using the energy, pop them in a dry pan on high heat and blast them, stirring, for a minute or two.

2 Pop the peanuts in a blender (you'll have to pulse them a few times and give the bowl a shake to loosen any bits that get stuck around the blade) or food processor if you have a fancy whizzy one, or bash them in a pestle and mortar, or, if you're low-tech, fling them into a freezer bag and bash them with a rolling pin. Whatever floats your nut-boat, you just need to crush them to smithereens.

3 Tip the crushed nuts into a large mixing bowl, and add both kinds of flour and the yeast and the salt (salt can be omitted if you are cooking for children or are watching your intake, I don't add it to much except the occasional bread and usually a little to stocks and sauces). Stir the dry ingredients to evenly distribute them.

4 Make a well (a kind of hole) in the centre of the dry ingredients. Add the oil, then most of the water – it should be just warm to touch, if it's too hot it murders the poor living yeast and then your bread won't work. Mix it in well to form a soft dough, adding the rest of the water if it needs it. Your dough should collect all of the flour from around the bowl, but not be too tacky – it shouldn't leave a residue on your hands. If it's too dry and cracking, add a splash more water. If you overdo the water, shake a little more flour in.

5 Tip it onto a well-floured work surface and knead well for a few minutes until it is soft and springy. Kneading is basically stretching it out with your palm and knuckles, folding it in half, giving it a quarter-turn and repeating. And repeating. And repeating, until it is bouncy. Don't throw it on the floor to test, just gently prod it with your finger to make an indent – it should slowly poof back out again.

6 Tip it back into the bowl and cover with cling film or a clean tea towel, and pop it somewhere warm for 1 hour to rise. If your home is chilly, or you can't find a warm place, pop a few tea towels in the microwave for a minute then wrap them around your bowl to give it a big warm cuddle.

7 When the dough has almost doubled in size, preheat the oven to 180°C/350°F/gas 4. Tip out the dough onto a floured worktop again and shape into a loaf – this will help knock out some of the extra air, but don't fiddle with it too much, as that air will contribute to a nice light loaf with a wonderful texture. Flour the baking tray and pop the dough onto it. Cut down the middle a centimetre or so deep with a knife (to let the baking fairies out, according to Irish folklore) and bake for 40 minutes. You'll know it's done when it feels light to hold, warm, hollow-sounding when you tap the bottom, and your home smells like freshly baked bread.

BREAKFASTS

It is often said that breakfast is the most important meal of the day, and yet, how often I either skip it in the mêlée of getting out of the front door on the school run, or shovel an unsatisfying half bowl of tasteless cereal down my neck as I flail about for shoes and basic hygiene and almost-matching socks. In my ideal world, breakfast would be a leisurely affair, with most of my five-a-day included, ensconced in a duvet fort with endless cups of tea and several newspapers. In reality, it's a banana blackening in the bottom of a handbag, or yesterday's cement porridge reheated and thoroughly chewed.

These recipes are for a range of circumstances, as morning routines will not be one-size-fits-all, but hopefully there's something you fancy, even just once in a while. The recipes range from the simple to the sumptuous, the speedy to the supine, and, mostly, they are what I dream of while fishing a smashed-up digestive biscuit from my gritty pocket on the way out of the school gates.

PING PORRIDGE (V)

SERVES 1

40g porridge oats

milk, for topping up (optional)

sugar, to taste (optional)

All you need for ping porridge – so-called because it can be done in the microwave, on the move, and is perfect in its portability – is a Tupperware-style container with a lid, a permanent marker and some oats. The adornments and accoutrements from there on are up to you. I find a taller container best for this, for accuracy, but if you don't mind a squat take-away carton or similar, use whatever you prefer.

I like to add apple and ground cinnamon to my porridge in the colder months, or dark chocolate and a few frozen berries, or tinned pears. Have fun with it – use it as a base and play with it as much or as little as you like.

1 Tip the oats into your container. Give them a gentle shake to level them out, then draw a firm line on the outside of the container at the top of the oats.

2 Add 200ml cold water, then draw a second line to indicate where the new level comes to. These two lines will be your secret breakfast weapon from hereon in, making it easier to pull this porridge together in a hurry, with no weighing needed. Pop the lid on loosely, and microwave at full blast for 90 seconds. Remove carefully, give it a stir, leave it to stand for a minute, then return it to the microwave for another minute.

3 Top up with milk if you like that kind of thing, a little sugar if you want it sweeter, and away you go: instant porridge, every day if you want it, a sight cheaper than the little packets you can buy individually portioned.

BERRY GREEN SMOOTHIE (V)

SERVES 1

20g porridge oats

200ml whole milk or equivalent non-dairy milk

70g frozen berries

25g frozen spinach (or as much or as little as you can stomach)

a drop of honey or golden syrup, to help the medicine go down

Now don't be put off by how wholesome this sounds, as it is a great – and cheap – little pick-me-up for those days where you just need to get something good inside. Hangovers, late nights, exhaustion, heavy colds, you know the sort. This is one of those recipes where the cheaper ingredients are the infinitely more superior ones, as frozen berries and frozen spinach make for a much better smoothie experience. When I have made a smoothie that has turned out to be a little less gratifying than I wanted it to be, most of the time it just needed to be a little colder, so start here and add what you like. (Pictured overleaf.)

1 Fling all of the ingredients into a blender – if you're using fresh berries and spinach instead of frozen, you may want to add a little ice. Pulse it a few times to break everything down, then blend on full power for just under a minute. If you like your smoothies super-smooth, you may want to add a dash of water and blend it again. You'll know it's done when there are no discernible pieces of spinach suspended in the rich purpley goodness.

2 Pour it into a glass and drink it quickly; smoothies have a tendency to separate if you leave them too long, so they are at their best straight from the blender jug. It's so purple, you shouldn't even notice the sneaky greens.

CRAPPUCCINO (V)

SERVES 1

30g porridge oats

250ml whole milk or equivalent non-dairy milk

a handful of ice cubes

1 tsp–1 tbsp instant coffee (according to personal taste)

1 tsp–1 tbsp sugar or honey (according to personal taste)

In my errant and often wayward youth, I worked at a well-known coffee chain, making endless coffee-based drinks for busy people with enough spare change to drop my hourly wage on a muffin and a sugary drink. I learned to make the perfect espresso, how to deep-clean a variety of complex machines, and that coffee is as complex and diverse as wine. And come the summer, I learned how to make a dozen milkshakes – or 'ice-blended drinks' – at a time, fast. It sometimes surprises me, the elements of my past lives that I pull into the present, but my love for a coffee-based thick milkshake has held fast, and when in a rush, it's the perfect grab-and-go breakfast for busy mornings. This isn't a replica of said coffee chain's version, not having access to their pasteurised cartons of sugar-and-badness, nor any burning desire to engage in legal proceedings, but it is a nod backwards to my younger self, and a wry recognition that some things never really change.

You can use this as a base to make it into whatever you like; I sometimes add a little cocoa powder or grated plain chocolate to mine, or a squidge of caramel ice-cream sauce, a pinch of vanilla seeds or orange zest. Go wild – you're basically having dessert for breakfast anyway, so you might as well go all out!

1 **Tip the oats into a blender. Add the milk, ice, coffee and sugar or honey.**

2 **Put the lid on the blender and pulse it a few times (that is, blitz it on full power for a few seconds at a time) until well combined. Give it a good shake, and pulse again if you need to. If it is a little too stiff to manage, loosen it with a drop of water or a little more milk.**

3 **Pour it into a glass, or portable cup, and off you go.**

BEETROOT, CARROT AND GINGER JUICE (WITHOUT A JUICER) (VE)

MAKES 2 GENEROUS GLASSES

1 raw or cooked beetroot (not the kind in vinegar)

1 large carrot or 2 rather small ones – or an apple, if you prefer

a small piece of fresh root ginger

½ lemon or 1 tbsp lemon juice – adjust to taste

a few pinches of turmeric

Hot off the back of my Beetballs (see page 176), I was looking for new and exciting ways to use my new favourite purple vegetable, so I threw it into a morning juice. I don't have a juicer, so instead I chucked it into my blender (admittedly a good little number, but that's because it gets used ten times a day, so any blender will do). Making juice without a juicer is simple, you are essentially pulverising your chosen fruits and vegetables in a jug blender with water, then straining it through a sieve, clean cloth or tea strainer to make juice. No bulky bastard-to-clean juicer required, just a blender, something to strain it through and a spoon. Voilà!

I could bang on about why I've chosen the ingredients that I have here, but basically it boils down to the simple 'I think juice is nice'. Ginger, lemon and turmeric help fight a cold, the beetroot is for the colour, the carrot for sweetness. I like juice.

1 Dice all of the ingredients, including the lemon if you are using a fresh one, rind and all, carefully picking out the seeds. You want the shoots and skins of your beetroot and the tops of your carrots, too, don't waste a thing. Lob everything into the blender and cover with 300–400ml cold water, then pulse to a bright purple liquid.

2 Place the tea strainer or a sieve over a jug, and if you like, line it with a clean non-fluffy tea towel or piece of muslin. Pour in the juice and allow to strain. If you are simply using a strainer, stir briskly with a teaspoon to disturb the pulp and extract the maximum juices – a human equivalent of the scary bit in the middle of a newfangled juicer. If you have lined it with a cloth, lift the fabric by the edges and corners, and allow the juice to drip out – you can squeeze it a little to speed up the process if you like, but clean your hands with lemon juice afterwards to get rid of the purple hue from the beetroots.

3 Reserve the pulp – it can be used in a variety of recipes, including those Beetballs, as a base for risotto, mix it with a tin of tomatoes and a hefty pinch of salt and chilli flakes for a pasta sauce to smuggle past fussy children and adults alike or add stock to it and make it into soup. Pour out and enjoy.

TIPS

● If you want to keep this drink for later, it's light and oxidisation that causes juices to discolour, so store them in a non-clear bottle like a Thermos flask or similar, in the fridge, and consume the next day. I tend to just drink the lot, and sod it.

● I like to keep a box of disposable gloves in my kitchen for handling beetroot, but they do attract some interesting comments from visitors.

SATURDAY MORNING PANCAKES (V)

**350g self-raising
flour**

**1 tsp bicarbonate
of soda**

**½ tsp salt, plus extra
for sprinkling**

**50g granulated
sugar, plus extra for
sprinkling**

**75g butter or 75ml
oil (not olive oil), plus
extra for frying**

**600ml whole milk or
equivalent non-dairy
milk**

**2 medium or large
eggs**

**1 x 410g tin of peach
slices in fruit juice**

**a pinch of salt and a
bit of cracked black
pepper**

**soft cream cheese,
to serve**

1 tbsp honey

**a pinch of finely
chopped fresh basil
or mint**

Saturday pancakes in bed is something of a tradition in my house – it's an unspoken 'I love you'; the graceless deposition of a stack of twelve fluffy clouds of goodness onto the pillow with a pair of forks and a jug of something hot and steamy to drown them in. Of course, you can make them any day of the week, but a lazy weekend morning to luxuriate over them is pretty damn perfect.

I confess to borrowing half of the ingredients list from *Masterchef*'s John Torode, on the BBC Good Food website, because sometimes no matter how good you think you are, someone else is always going to be better – and life is too short for sub-par breakfasts. The honeyed, roasted peaches and accoutrements and flowery, overlong, wittering recipe, however, are all my own work.

1 First combine the flour, bicarb, salt and sugar, stirring well to evenly distribute them – you don't want to end up with one super-fluffy pancake and the rest sad, flat and claggy. Therein lie the seeds of a family mutiny, and nobody wants one of those on the weekend.

2 Sling the butter into a microwave-safe bowl and ping it on a medium heat for 30 seconds to soften it if it is at room temperature, 60 seconds if straight from the fridge. (It's never around long enough in my house to go bad, so I leave my butter out on the side, but you probably shouldn't.) If you don't have a microwave, melt it in a small pan for a minute and remove it when it's nice and sloppy.

3 Add half the milk to the dry ingredients and mix well to form a stiff paste. Loosen it with half of the remaining milk, and repeat until all the milk is used up. Resist the temptation to sling it in all at once; you'll end up with either lumpy batter or a sore arm from beating it out. Add the melted butter or oil and mix it in thoroughly, then stir in the eggs and pop the whole lot in the fridge for at least half an hour for a little chill-out. The best pancakes are the ones with slightly crisp edges and fat, featherlight middles, and the best way to achieve this is to pour freezing cold batter into a shit-hot pan and wait for science to do the rest.

4 While the batter chills out, preheat the oven to 180°C/350°F/gas 4. Drain the peaches, reserving the juice for an accompanying drink or slutty bellini, and tip the fruit into an ovenproof dish. Very lightly salt them, dust with sugar and roast for 30 minutes – conveniently the same amount of time the pancake batter needs to chill for … it's almost as though I've done this before! Leave the oven on to keep the pancakes warm as you make them.

5 When the batter is nice and chilled, heat the largest frying pan you can find. Dollop in a little butter or oil, and crank that heat up until it's toasty warm but not smoking. Please don't let it smoke, that's how kitchen fires start, so if it does start kicking off, remove it from the heat immediately and set it down on a heatproof surface to completely cool, then rinse out the ruined fat and start again. I wish someone had told me this a long time ago, so I'm telling you now. I digress. Back to pancakeville we go.

6 When your pan is nice and warm and definitely not on fire, dollop a hefty spoon of mixture into it, and another one, and another one. Cook for a few minutes before deftly turning them over with a palette knife or spatula, and cook for a few minutes more. You'll need to do these in batches, so remove them onto a baking tray or sheet and pop them in the bottom of the oven while you cook up the remaining batter. If you suspect this may take a while, turn the oven down to 120°C/250°F/gas ½ to keep them warm but not eventually chargrilled!

7 When all the batter is used up, pop your pancakes on a large plate (or a few smaller ones if you're territorial about your breakfast). Dollop on the soft cream cheese, tip over the peaches, drizzle the lot in honey, and finish with a smattering of sugar, a crack of black pepper, and some finely chopped basil or mint. Take back to bed, bunch your duvet around your waist, and enjoy.

FLUFFY BERRY PANCAKES (V)

SERVES 2

2 tsp butter

150g plain flour

1 tsp bicarbonate of soda

1 tbsp granulated sugar

80ml milk

2 medium or large eggs

100g frozen berries

oil, for greasing

golden syrup or honey, to serve

These are a favourite of my Small Boy, and something of a lazy Sunday morning tradition. We pop to the shop with our coats on over our pyjamas, grab a newspaper for me and a comic for him, and loaf around with all the breakfast we can possibly manage, reading, chatting and making up for a week of hastily bolted porridge and cartons of juice on the run to school. Breakfast rolls into lunch, into walks, into movies, into catching up with friends, but a Sunday isn't a Sunday without a pancake in our house. Vegan readers, you can replace eggs with 2 over-ripe mashed bananas, and butter with a little oil.

This recipe is easily multiplied for larger crowds, in which case pop a couple of baking trays in the oven as it preheats to around 140°C/275°F/gas 1, and use them to keep the pancakes warm as you cook. It's no fun being the person with the cold pancakes at the breakfast table.

1 First pop the butter in a microwave-proof dish and melt for a few seconds. Set to one side, and work quickly.

2 Pour the flour, bicarb and sugar into a bowl and mix well to combine. Make a well (a big wide dent) in the middle of the dry ingredients and pour in the milk and melted butter. Crack in the eggs and mix it all together to make your pancake mix.

3 Now let it rest. This is important, and helps create the lightest, fluffiest pancakes. The best place to rest it is in the fridge, as science dictates that cold batter meeting hot oil is the optimum for an air, perfect reaction. And I generally don't question science when cooking, as it knows more than I do. So pop it in the fridge and spend half an hour doing something else entirely.

4 When the batter is rested, remove it from the fridge, tip in the berries, and give it a quick stir. Grab a frying pan, preferably a non-stick one, and brush it with a little oil. Bring it to a high heat for a minute to warm the pan through, but don't let the oil start smoking, so watch it. Reduce the heat to medium, and dollop in some pancake mixture. The first one is always the worst – a snack for the hard-working chef is my rule! Cook for 1 minute and then, using a spatula, gently turn it over. Repeat until all of the pancake batter is used up, and serve in a stack, hot, with something runny and sweet.

COOKING ON A BOOTSTRAP

MICROWAVE KALE AND CHILLI EGGS (V)

SERVES 1

a small handful of kale, spinach or spring greens

a pinch of chilli flakes

1 x 200g tin of chopped tomatoes

a pinch of salt and a bit of cracked black pepper

1 tsp lemon juice, fresh or bottled

2 eggs

Kale suddenly burst into fashion a few years ago; a large, dark green leaf once grown to feed cattle with, was suddenly everywhere. Food writers were falling over themselves – myself included – to make this bitter brassica into something palatable for the masses. I shoved it in a pesto, as most greens come into their own with a hefty dose of fat, lemon, salt and cheese, and the odd risotto, a ribollita and let it swim in a soup or two. Kale generally requires a good deal of cooking to soften it (I'm afraid I will never be one of those people who can drink it raw in a smoothie, I can detect the tiniest bit of it from miles away), but this recipe is an exception, as the microwave does all of the hard work for you. I came up with this one when I was living in a bedsit with no oven, and just a microwave and kettle to cook with, and it became one of my favourite simple meals at the time.

1 In a microwaveable bowl, mix the kale, chilli and chopped tomatoes with the salt and the lemon juice. Push the mixture to the sides of the bowl to make a well in the middle.

2 Separate the eggs – whites in one bowl and yolks in the other, as eggs can be volatile under pressure, and the yolk tends to cook faster than the white, which isn't ideal at all. Tip the egg whites into the centre of the tomato mixture. Cover the bowl with cling film and cook on a medium setting in the microwave for 40 seconds, then allow to cool for a moment before heating for another 40 seconds.

3 Add the egg yolks to the partially cooked whites, then gently pierce the yolk of each one to break the membrane – to prevent them from exploding. Microwave for another 40 seconds, then remove. Leave for 30 seconds for the hot spots to settle, then carefully peel back the cling film, starting with the edge furthest away from you to stop yourself from getting a faceful of hot steam. Grind over some black pepper, and serve.

MANDARIN BIRCHER (V)

SERVES 2

1 apple, any kind

50g porridge oats

200g natural yoghurt

1 x 298g tin of mandarins in fruit juice

a drizzle of honey or golden syrup

a handful of nuts or seeds (optional)

Birchers are like an effortless overnight porridge, knocked together and left to luxuriate in the fridge until a handful of simple ingredients swell into soft, sloppy oats, sweetened with a little fruit, and ideal for a quick breakfast at home or on the go. I make mine with frozen berries sometimes (as seen in *A Year in 120 Recipes*), or pears and wintery spices around Christmas time, but in summer mandarin bircher is very much in vogue in my house. In style, that is. Not the magazine. I'll eat my own hat if I ever appear in the latter.

Traditional bircher has an apple grated into the bottom of it, but we rarely have apples kicking around in this house, so you can take it or leave it. I smuggle it in when I remember, just as an extra portion of fruit to get into the Small Boy without much of a fuss.

1 First grate the apple into the bottom of a large mixing bowl, then quickly cover it with the oats – doing this straight away keeps the air out and stops the tiny pieces of apple going brown (enzymic browning – caused when oxygen comes into contact with fruit, and about all I can remember from my school Science lessons. I never imagined it would come in handy, but life is strange and wonderful). Add the yoghurt and mix everything together.

2 Drain the mandarins to separate the juice from the fruit, reserving the juice, then add half the mandarin segments to the bowl. Pour the fruit juice into a measuring jug and add enough cold water to make the liquid up to 150ml. If you don't have a measuring jug, a standard-sized mug holds around 300ml water, so make it about half of one of those. (And think about treating yourself to a measuring jug; some hardware stores sell plastic ones for around 25p, and I pooh-poohed having one for years, but they are genuinely useful.) Pour the measured liquid over the oat and apple mix.

3 Find two small jars, bowls or ramekins and evenly spoon the bircher mix into them. Add the remaining mandarins on top, drizzle with honey or syrup, and sprinkle with the nuts or seeds, if you're using them. Pop the pots in the fridge overnight, or for at least 4 hours, and enjoy within 2 days.

MARMALADE GRANOLA (V)

MAKES 8 SERVINGS

1–2 tbsp butter or oil, plus extra for greasing

4 tbsp marmalade

4 tbsp honey or golden syrup

300g porridge oats

Regular readers of my recipes will know that I am a fan of a granola, having made a fair few over the years. Peanut butter granola for the *Guardian*, apple crumble granola on my online blog, and various others in my kitchen, all bottled up in large jars for when the need for a good munch and crunch strikes. I feel a little like a cereal-based Robin Hood, swiping the fancy ideas from their recycled boxes in the health-food aisles and recreating them in a sticky, naughty, straightforward and inexpensive way for the masses. And they don't get much simpler than this one. Sometimes when I'm feeling particularly irreverent I add a handful of plain chocolate, chipped into pieces, too. It's like legitimate Jaffa Cakes for breakfast.

1 Preheat the oven to 180°C/350°F/gas 4. Lightly grease a baking tray. Melt the butter or oil, marmalade and honey or syrup together in a large pan over low heat, or in a microwave-safe bowl in the microwave on medium power for 1 minute. Stir well to combine.

2 When it has all melted together, tip in the oats. Stir well – hence using a large pan – making sure they are evenly coated. Some of the oats will start to clump together at this stage – this is brilliant, don't try to break them up too much!

3 Tip the mixture onto the baking tray, spreading it out to help it cook evenly. Place the tray carefully in the centre of the oven and bake for 20 minutes. Reduce the heat to 160°C/325°F/gas 3 and cook for a further 10 minutes. Then remove from the oven and allow to cool completely – around 30 minutes to 1 hour.

4 Transfer the granola to a clean large jar or container, where it will keep for around 3 months at room temperature.

SHAKSHUKA (V)

SERVES 2, IF YOU'RE
IN A SHARING MOOD

1 onion, finely sliced

**1 pepper of any
colour, deseeded and
finely sliced**

1 tbsp oil

**2 tsp cumin, seeds
or ground**

**a pinch of salt and a
bit of cracked black
pepper**

**1 x 400g tin of
chopped tomatoes**

**a handful of spinach
or other leafy greens
(for brownie points)**

2–4 eggs

**a pinch of chilli or
paprika, or both**

I first had shakshuka the morning after a very heavy night before, with a friend who had come to rescue me from the vulgarities of my own hangover in the middle of London. He took me to a café, ordered me shakshuka, and watched, giggling to himself, as I slowly turned from a mumbling wreck into something that vaguely resembled a human being. I have made and loved it many times since, usually in varying degrees of unwellness, both self-inflicted and unfortunately less so. If you need any further convincing, it packs a vitamin C punch from the peppers and tomatoes, and the spices will wake you up and clear out any lurking nasties. As for the egg? Eggs are good for pretty much everything. (Vegans, replace the egg with a tin of chickpeas for the same protein hit but a completely different dish!)

Recipe continues overleaf

1 Chuck the onion and pepper into a pan with the oil, cumin, salt and pepper. Cook on medium heat until the onions have started to soften, then pour over the tomatoes. Slice and add the greens, if using them. Cook for around 10 minutes, stirring occasionally to disturb everything so it doesn't stick and burn.

2 Crank the heat up high and add a splash of water to loosen the mixture, as the eggs need something to cook in. Kind of like poaching, but not like poaching, because I can't poach an egg to save my life, hence always cooking them in fancy ways like this. It's not because I'm actually fancy, it's because some of the most basic cooking skills are my Achilles heel, and I'm probably never going to get them right. Mix it all well.

3 When it starts to bubble and splutter, make a gap in the mixture and break in the eggs, one at a time. Cook them for a minute or two, then reduce the heat to medium. Cover the pan (with a lid, tin foil, plate, anything but your hands) and cook for around 5 minutes, peeking halfway through to see that the white is cooked but the yolk is still runnyish with a promise of soft sloppy gorgeousness. Serve, like so many of my recipes, immediately with a sprinkle of chilli or paprika and a good pinch or grind of black pepper.

TIP

● To make this more substantial, you can serve it on toast, or in a stack of toast, or if you're impressing someone, grab a small crusty bread roll, gently lop the top inch off, pull out all the bread, and scoop your hot sloppy spicy egg into it to serve. I have done this. They were impressed. I feel duty-bound to pass on these ninja skills. However you serve it, enjoy it – that's the main thing!

GRAMCAKE (VE)

SERVES 2

75g gram flour

a pinch of salt and a bit of black pepper or chilli flakes

a splash of oil, for frying

Also known as 'socca' or 'farinata' in some places, a gramcake is a pancake made with just one ingredient – gram flour. Gram flour is admittedly a bit of a specialist ingredient, but I keep it around for this, a quick breakfast or lunch on the go that you just add water to. It can be made into a pizza base (see page 34), or jazzed up with herbs and spices, eaten hot or cold, used as a wrap (if you manage to get it thin enough), or as a vehicle for scooping up last night's take-away curry. You can find gram flour in the World Foods section of most larger supermarkets, or at most ethnic supermarkets and large corner shops. It's also useful for thickening sauces, binding falafels and bhajis, padding out a hummus, and I once found a rather intriguing recipe for gram flour fudge.

You can spice this up however you like. Depending on my mood, sometimes I sling a bit of turmeric or paprika in, sometimes cumin, sometimes some thyme or rosemary, and sometimes a mixture of all of them. You can't really go wrong with this one, so half a teaspoon of whatever you fancy will do it good.

1 Put the gram flour and 150ml cold water together in a mug and beat briskly with a fork to get any lumps out. This may take some doing; sometimes I sift it first, especially if the bag has been open a while, as it can be a little stubborn when exposed to moisture. If all else fails, you can sift out the lumps after you get fed up with beating it, and just discard them. Life is, after all, short.

2 Season it with a little salt and pepper, and any spices you want to add. Now pop it in the fridge for at least half an hour to chill and thicken. This step is vital, and without it you won't have a gramcake but you will have a disappointment. Go and do something else and forget all about it for a bit.

3 When it has chilled out for a while (and, hopefully, so have you!), heat a not-too-big frying pan with a little oil in it. Drop in a speck of the mixture to see if the oil is hot enough; if it sizzles, you're good to go. Pour in half of the mug and let it cook for a minute or two before turning down the heat. I'm useless at tossing pancakes so I place a large pan lid over it to cook the top side instead of risking a flip, but it's up to you! Either way, cook it for a few minutes on each side, before transferring it to a plate to cool. I like to place a piece of kitchen roll or greaseproof paper on my plate to soak up any excess oil from the first one, but it's not essential. I just learned it in professional kitchens and now I can't seem to break the habit.

4 Make the second one the same way as the first, and when they're done, serve with a flourish. Top with natural yoghurt, mango chutney, leftover curry, or just roll it up and stuff it into your gob.

MICROWAVE MOUNTAIN OMELETTE (V)

SERVES 2

4 large eggs

2 spring onions or 1 small onion, finely chopped

a couple of pickled jalapeno peppers, finely chopped, or a pinch of chilli flakes (optional)

a pinch of salt and a bit of cracked black pepper

a good grating of any kind of cheese (optional, but delicious)

I first made this mound of goodness in Budapest, Hungary, where my tiny but beautiful briefly rented apartment came equipped with a crabby old plastic microwave, two IKEA mugs, a couple of teaspoons and a knife that hadn't seen a sharpener (or possibly even another human being) since Take That were a five-piece. The corner shop stocked loose vegetables and hostility, so I picked up a couple of spring onions, a few eggs and some pickled jalapeno peppers for less than the price of a cup of tea back home. Whenever I find myself writing or reporting abroad, I like to grab a handful of something from the nearest shop and turn it into a meal, partly because I enjoy thinking on my feet, partly so that I can explore the local produce, and partly because if I spend more than 48 hours outside of a kitchen I become crotchety, cabin-feverish and mildly insane.

Jalapenos can be quite a specialist ingredient, depending on whether you have a nacho habit or not (guilty, Your Honour), so if they aren't the kind of thing you keep kicking about the place, feel free to replace them with a regular chilli or a dash of hot sauce or Tabasco. Any heat will do. You can double or triple the recipe to feed as many people as you need to; I can fit seven mugs on my microwave plate with a little jostling, but the more you pack into your microwave, the longer cooking time it needs. Those lively little particles can only do so much, you know.

1 Take two microwave-safe mugs (non-metal), crack 2 eggs into each and beat well. Split the onions and jalapeno (if using) evenly between the mugs, with a little salt and pepper, and mix to combine. Remove the fork and set it to one side.

2 Pop the mugs in the microwave. Set it to medium heat and cook for 90 seconds.

3 Remove carefully, and beat the mixture in each mug well with the fork. The microwave will typically cook the top first so the mixture needs a thorough beating to break it up and cook evenly. Return to the microwave for a further 90 seconds.

4 Remove again, and if you are adding cheese, now would be the time to do it. Toss it in and ping the microwave for another 90 seconds.

5 Now it should be done, but not all microwaves are created equal, so you'll need to be a little liberal with your timings here. If, once removed, the omelette is firm and no longer sloppy, you're good to go. If it is still a little wet, beat it again and return to the microwave for 90 seconds more.

6 When finished, gently run a knife or spoon around the inside edge of the mug to loosen it, and turn it out slowly onto your plate. Done well, it will form a slightly shaky mountain of cheesy eggy goodness. Done haphazardly, as half of mine are, you get some hot, spicy, soft, delicious scrambled eggs. Either way, you're winning. I serve mine on top of either bread, toast or a pile of finely chopped greens, depending on what I have to hand and how wholesome I feel.

COURGETTE LEMON PANCAKES (V)

SERVES 2 (MAKES 4)

1 decent-sized courgette (around 300g)

juice and zest of ½ lemon or 1 tbsp bottled lemon juice

125g gram flour

1 medium egg

a pinch of chilli flakes or cracked black pepper

a pinch of salt

oil, for frying

soft cheese or natural yoghurt, to serve

This is much the same as the humble gramcake, but a little more substantial. I often get readers asking me what they should do with courgettes, and being a polite girl, I'm inclined to give an answer of the culinary variety. Come the summer, it seems as though everyone and their allotment has a glut of courgettes going begging, and if you don't know anyone who grows them, they're pretty cheap to buy.

1 Line a large bowl with a clean tea towel or a few sheets of kitchen roll, and grate the courgette into it. Use the tea towel or kitchen roll to wring out excess moisture over the sink, then return the courgette to the bowl.

2 Add the lemon juice, and then the gram flour, and give it all a good mix to coat the courgettes fairly evenly.

3 Add 125ml cold water and mix well, then add another 125ml and mix again. Add the egg and toss in the lemon zest (if using) and chilli or pepper, and the salt. Give it one last stir, and pop it in the fridge for at least half an hour.

4 When it is chilled, warm a large non-stick frying pan over high heat with a little oil for a minute. Turn the heat down to medium, and pour in a quarter of the batter. Cover the pan with a large lid (any pan lid will do, if it's a little too big it doesn't matter), or a dinner plate, and cook for a few minutes until the underside starts to set. If the top is covered, this will start to set, too.

5 Very, very carefully, using a spatula, remove the pancake and turn it over. Cook for a few more minutes on the other side, before removing and setting to one side. At this point I generally turn the oven on with a lightly greased baking sheet in it, at 120°C/250°F/gas ½, to keep them warm while I cook the rest. Or you could have four frying pans on the go – but I don't even own four frying pans and I do this for a living!

6 Repeat until all of the mixture is gone, and you should have four decent-sized and delicious lemony courgette pancakes. Top with soft cheese or natural yoghurt, or any cheese, or anything you like, really.

PIZZA TOAST (V)

SERVES 2

2 tbsp tomato purée

2 thick slices of bread, a chunk of baguette cut in half, or a muffin or crumpet

a handful of strong cheese

any toppings you require: onion, mushroom, peppers, tomatoes – you choose!

Pizza toast is another relic from my youth, when I would spend my Thursday evenings helping out at my local Girls Brigade, at the Baptist church over the road. Those of you who know me these days may raise an eyebrow at the heavily tattooed, sweary lesbian being a fledgling leader of ministry, but there I was, sleeves rolled up, happy to help. Cooking in the huge church kitchen, with its stainless-steel worktops and double-handled pans that you felt could literally feed the five thousand, was a rare treat, and unsurprisingly, one I approached with boundless enthusiasm. We would make peppermint creams, the odd fairy cake, poke pineapples and silverskin onions onto cocktail sticks, and feel ever so grown up in the process. And there was always 'pizza'. Tomato purée and cheese slathered onto a crumpet, or a piece of French stick, or a slice of bread, and toasted. It wasn't really pizza at all, but it was a quick and simple snack for little hands. Pizza toast is one of the first things I taught my Small Boy to cook, and we still enjoy it today; it is as much of a treat to me now as it was all those years ago.

1 **Slather the tomato purée over the bread, top with cheese and your preferred toppings.**

2 **Cook under a hot grill for 5 minutes, until heated through and the cheese is bubbling and golden.**

FRENCH TOAST (V)

SERVES 2

1 egg

50ml milk (generous 3 tablespoons)

¼ tsp ground cinnamon

2 slices of bread

oil or butter, for frying

a little sugar, honey or golden syrup, to serve

French toast – also known as 'eggy bread', is an absolute classic, and mastering it is extremely simple. It's my Small Boy's favourite 'pity food', that is, the one he asks for when he is a little unwell, tired, or under the weather. A perfect balance of nursery-bland and mindlessly suckable softness, you can keep it as simple or make it as highfalutin as you like. Some days I serve it with a knob of butter and eat it from a bowl with a spoon, and other days I top it with a mound of hot berries (just frozen berries pinged in the microwave and drained of excess juices, but shhh, it looks like more effort than it ever was).

1 Grab a decent-sized mixing bowl and crack the egg into it. Beat with a fork until well combined. Add the milk and cinnamon and beat again.

2 Cut the bread in half – I like it in triangles, but admittedly rectangles are more practical to deal with, so do it however you fancy. Put the pieces of bread into the bowl and push them under the egg mixture to soak them thoroughly.

3 Take a frying pan, add a little oil or butter, and warm it on the hob on medium heat for a minute. Carefully add the bread – as many slices as will comfortably fit – and cook for around 5 minutes until the underside starts to brown. Using tongs, a fork, or a spatula, carefully turn it over and cook the other side for a few minutes more.

4 When cooked, gently lift your French toast onto a plate. Sprinkle with a little sugar (or honey or syrup, if you fancy) and eat it while it's hot!

SOUPS

Soup is one of my favourite midway meals; it can be light, or seriously hearty and filling. It is the place for using scrappy tired vegetables lolling about in the bottom of the fridge – an almost Biblical miracle whereby one tin of beans can stretch to feeding four people. It can be repurposed as a pasta sauce, used as the base for a risotto or frozen for that day when you don't fancy cooking.

Good soup feels like a maternal, comforting hug, and once you have the hang of it, you can soup almost anything. I make soups from yellow-sticker bargains at my local supermarket, leftovers and odds and ends. Protein-packed, thick ones are my favourites – sling a tin of beans in for a seriously filling lunch.

It's worth investing in a blender to make the most of bargains and leftovers; a basic jug blender from supermarkets' own ranges will set you back a tenner and last a couple of years. If you can't stretch to one, mash soups to a purée with a fork or potato masher, or leave it chunky. The flavours will turn out the same.

WORTS

SERVES 2, EASILY
DOUBLED

**1 onion, of any size or
colour, thinly sliced**

a splash of oil

100g porridge oats

**1 chicken or
vegetable stock cube
dissolved in 400ml
boiling water**

100g frozen spinach

**1 tbsp lemon juice
or zest and juice of
½ lemon**

**chilli flakes or
cayenne pepper,
to taste**

**a pinch of salt and
grind of pepper**

I came across this curiosity while researching medieval cookery books in the vast and astonishing Reading Rooms at the British Library. The Reading Rooms have restricted access and contain thousands upon thousands of old, loved books and manuscripts, some of them centuries old. Cooking and eating are not new concepts, and neither is being strapped for cash, so I spent many long afternoons and evenings sitting at a large wooden desk, piles of history at my fingertips, to see what I could learn. This recipe cropped up in various places in its most basic form – as greens cooked with oats, in broth. I felt that the original version was a peasant-food step too far for most of us; the idea of 'spinach gruel' made even me a little sceptical. So I took the recipe home and tweaked it a little, and eventually settled on this creamy, nourishing, warming soup, created from a little frozen spinach and a handful of porridge oats.

For a creamier soup, make this with the same quantities of milk as the water and add a stock cube. For an alarmingly pink soup, add chunks of fresh beetroot. Use this as a base and play with it: who doesn't love an excuse to have a bowl of warming porridge – in any form?

1 Toss the onion into a saucepan with the oil. Cook on gentle heat for a few minutes to soften. Add the oats, stock and the frozen spinach and bring to the boil. Cook gently for around 15 minutes, until the oats swell and it all starts to thicken, then remove from the heat.

2 Pour into a blender with a splash of water and pulse until smooth. Tip back into the pan. Loosen with a little water if required – it should be the consistency of soup, rather than porridge, and not all oats are created equal.

3 Splash in the lemon juice, then add the chilli or cayenne pepper, and taste. Season as required, and enjoy. If you leave it to cool, it will solidify, as oats invariably do. Not to worry, it can be heated through with a little more water to return it to its soupy state, rather than a bar of solid greenish porridge.

MUSHROOM AND GREEK CHEESE SOUP

SERVES 4

1 onion, finely sliced

2 fat garlic cloves, finely sliced

2 tbsp oil

a pinch of salt and a bit of cracked black pepper

400g mushrooms

1 vegetable or chicken stock cube

100g feta or Greek salad cheese

100ml milk

a dash of any vinegar or lemon juice, fresh or bottled

One of my favourite ingredients from the value range at the supermarket is 'Greek-style cheese'. Like a feta, it is crumbly, salty and packs a real flavour punch for the price, which is an essential consideration when cooking on a budget. A little goes a long way, and it lends a creamy texture to soups and dips, making them taste comforting and luxurious. Even using basic mushrooms and cheap stock, this soup is so much more than the sum of its parts.

1 Toss the onion and garlic into a saucepan with the oil, a pinch of salt and a little pepper. Cook on gentle heat for around 5 minutes, just to knock the acerbic raw taste off the edges of the onion.

2 Slice or break up the mushrooms, knocking off any visible soil – I keep an old toothbrush by the kitchen sink for this very purpose, as they can be a little stubborn sometimes. I also snap my mushrooms in half by hand, because endlessly slicing things can be such a faff, and it's a rather nice stress release to just harmlessly, physically, break things from time to time. Try it and see, you might agree with me, but I don't think I've sliced a mushroom in years (nor broccoli, cauliflower, and similar). Add the mushrooms to the pan.

3 Add 500ml water to the pan and crumble in the stock cube, then bring to the boil. Crumble in the cheese. Cook for a further 10 minutes, then pour two-thirds of the soup into a blender. Remembering to put the lid on (a cautionary tale lurks between the lines here), pulse it to a smooth consistency.

4 Pour it back into the pan and cook for a further 10 minutes, thinning with 500ml water and the milk until it is the consistency you like it. Some people prefer their soups almost chewy, and some like to drink theirs from a mug, so there is no hard and fast rule.

5 Add a dash of vinegar or lemon juice to finish it, this brightens the flavour and is something I do for most of my dishes that contain rich, creamy flavours, so bear it in mind. Good old standard malt vinegar will do in lieu of anything more fancy. Enjoy!

ONE-INGREDIENT MUSHROOM SOUP (VE)

MAKES 2 GENEROUS PORTIONS

400g mushrooms of any variety

a small slug of oil

a pinch of salt and a bit of cracked black pepper

lemon juice to lift and brighten, fresh or bottled, or any kind of vinegar

This very simple recipe started as a ponder, a wonder, as so many of mine do. Mushrooms are cheap, easy to grow (if you have the inclination) and provide an incredible amount of bang for their buck. I keep my eyes peeled for cheap ones, especially the exotic varieties marked down at the end of the day, and dry them out to use at a later date. As a result, I often have a large jar or freezer bag of dried mushrooms kicking around, full of intense flavour, and I can luxuriate in the knowledge that they won't go bad any time soon.

This soup was born of a couple of boxes of aforementioned reduced mushrooms; delicate, long, skinny enoki, fat meaty shiitakes, fragile and ethereal oysters and the usual common or garden mushrooms found in the cheaper ranges at the supermarket. It will work with any mushrooms, so don't feel obliged to seek out the posher varieties, that's not the point of this book, after all. The key here is long and slow – ideal if you have a small slow cooker, but if not, a saucepan will do. It doubles up as a creamy base for a simple risotto, or as a pasta sauce.

Feel free to play with herbs, cheese, chilli – customise it as you will, but here's the body of it to start you off. You can add dried mushrooms, for a deeper flavour, or a handful of herbs at the beginning. Rosemary would complement the earthiness of the mushrooms, as would thyme. Ordinary mixed dried herbs in a jar would work just fine, too. Fresh parsley and coriander are brighter herbs, so if you feel it needs a lift or a little less seriousness, give them a go. Use it as a base and toy with it. And, of course, if you want to add a splash of milk, cream or coconut cream to temper and soften it, feel free. A handful of oats at the beginning would do the same job. Basically, run with it. Cooking should be an adventure, so be as bold or as simple as you want to be.

1 Grab your mushrooms and give them a quick clean to remove any obvious lumps of earth; I keep a cheap toothbrush by the sink for this very purpose and just run it over them dry, but a clean, rough tea towel will do the same job.

2 Break up the mushrooms – I find snapping them with my hands far more efficient than painstakingly slicing them up – and pop them into a decent-sized pan with the oil over medium heat. Cook for around 10 minutes, stirring occasionally to stop them from sticking and burning.

3 Add 500ml water and crank up the heat to bring it to the boil. Season with a little salt and pepper, not too much, as you can always add more later but it's hard to fish out if you go too heavy to begin with! Reduce to a simmer and cook at this heat for around 30 minutes. The water should turn an ominous, dark chestnutty brown. It doesn't look like much at the moment, but stay with it.

4 Remove the pan from the heat and tip into your blender, then blend until smooth. If it's too thick, add a splash more water.

5 Pour it back into the pan and cook for another 10 minutes to reduce slightly. Taste it, and add salt, pepper and lemon juice or a dash of vinegar according to your preferences. If it seems a little bland, there's nothing a good squeeze of lemon won't liven up. (I pretty much live by a dash of lemon and a pinch of salt to jazz up anything that seems a little lacking.) And there you have it, an extraordinarily simple mushroom soup.

CHEESE SOUP

**1 large onion, finely
sliced**

**2 fat garlic cloves,
finely sliced**

2 tbsp butter or oil

1 tbsp flour

**1 chicken or
vegetable stock cube,
crumbled**

**400ml water, or
half-water, half-milk**

**a pinch of mixed
dried herbs or picked
fresh rosemary or
thyme leaves**

**200g strong cheese,
grated**

**a pinch of salt and a
bit of cracked black
pepper**

**a splash of vinegar or
lemon juice, fresh or
bottled**

This started as a request from my young son, then six years old, when he was feeling a little poorly one weekend and rather sorry for himself. I asked him what would make him feel better, keen to get some nourishing goodness into his small body to give him the strength to get well. It was just a heavy cold and a dose of self-pity, but when you're small, and even when you're not so small, illness can be frustrating and discombobulating. 'Cheese', came the reply. 'You can't just have cheese,' I laughed. 'How about some nice warm soup?' He pondered for a moment. 'Cheese soup?' And so cheese soup was born.

And, dear readers, it is intoxicating. It's essentially a sexed-up, watered-down, basic cheese sauce. The boy is a genius. I managed to sneak an onion into this one, as onions are full of goodness, but any mild vegetable would work as a base. Grated courgettes are good, as are carrots and cauliflower – it will all be blended up and smothered in cheese anyway, so smuggle in as much goodness as you can.

1 Toss the onion and garlic into a saucepan with the butter or oil. Cook gently on low heat to soften for a few minutes, stirring to disturb so they do not stick and burn.

2 Add the flour and crumbled stock cube, and mix well with a fork or wooden spoon to form a rough paste, then add a splash of the water or milk-water to loosen. Repeat, beating constantly to prevent any lumps forming. Continue until most of the liquid has been added, then bring to the boil. Add the herbs.

3 Add the grated cheese to the pan and stir well to melt it in. Cook for around 15 minutes to thicken and completely melt the cheese. Remove from the heat and pour into a blender. Pulse until smooth, then pour back into the pan to reheat. Season with salt and pepper, and a splash of vinegar or lemon juice to brighten it, and serve.

POOR CHAPLAIN SOUP

SERVES 2

4 large onions, finely sliced

oil or butter, for frying

1 tbsp plain flour

1 chicken or vegetable stock cube, crumbled

400ml water, or half-water, half-milk

a few stale bread crusts, or 1 slice

a splash of lemon juice, fresh or bottled

a handful of grated strong cheese

a good grind of black pepper

The original recipe that I found for this soup contained 'a hundred onions', with no clarification as to how many poor chaplains it was intended to feed. I decided to spare myself the bother of peeling and slicing a hundred onions, as it seemed a little excessive, and settled on a modest four. The original used milk in place of stock, but I don't have it in the house so often, so I make mine with stock.

1 Toss the onions into a saucepan with a little oil or butter. Cook on the lowest imaginable heat for around 20 minutes, stirring to disturb continuously, until the onions have softened and become translucent. Add the flour and stir well to coat them.

2 Add the crumbled stock cube, and mix well with a fork or wooden spoon to form a rough paste, then add a splash of the water or milk-water to loosen. Repeat, beating constantly to prevent any lumps forming. Continue until most of the liquid has been added, then bring to the boil. Reduce to a simmer and cook for around 30 minutes.

3 Tear up or slice the stale bread and add it to the pot along with the lemon juice. Cook for a further 10 minutes until soft and swollen.

4 Serve with a handful of grated cheese on top, allowing it to melt slightly, and a grind of black pepper. Fresh herbs are always welcome, and most work well with this. I have used rosemary, parsley and coriander, but a shake of mixed dried herbs is good, too.

COLCANNON SOUP

MAKES 2 GENEROUS,
COMFORTING
PORTIONS

a large onion or a few
spring onions, thinly
sliced

a knob of butter, or
more, for frying,
plus extra to serve

1 x 400g tin of new
potatoes in water

1 chicken or
vegetable stock cube
dissolved in 250ml
boiling water

250ml milk

2 large handfuls of
loose-leaf cabbage,
spring greens
or kale, roughly
chopped

a pinch of salt and
a bit of cracked
black pepper

I was raised on colcannon as a child, my Irish mother dolloping it on plates beside rashers of bacon and dousing the lot in gravy. It was only a matter of time before the leftovers manoeuvred themselves into a soup, and then developed into its own fit-for-purpose recipe. I keep some of the onions chunky, in keeping with the rough-and-tumble texture of a good colcannon. I make this for myself when I am unwell sometimes, as it comfortingly reminds me of my childhood, holidays in Ireland and my dear Granny Beatty.

1 Toss the onion into a medium saucepan. Add the butter and cook gently on low heat for a few minutes to soften. Remove half of the onions with a slotted spoon onto a plate and set to one side.

2 Open the tin of potatoes, drain them and give them a quick spritz under the tap to get rid of the tinny taste they acquire. Chop them up roughly and tip them into the pot. Add the stock and bring to the boil, then reduce the heat and simmer for around 10 minutes. The potatoes will need scant cooking, as they are already cooked, but a little softening and some flavour is required.

3 Tip the whole lot into a blender. Add the milk, and whizz until smooth. Pour back into the pan and warm through gently to stop the milk curdling. Drop in the reserved onions and the greens. Stir to wilt the greens, season with salt to taste, and serve with a dollop of butter and a pinch of pepper to finish.

PAYN FONDUE

SERVES 2

1 large onion, finely sliced

oil or butter, for frying

a piece of stale bread

200ml red wine

1 chicken, beef or vegetable stock cube dissolved in 200ml boiling water

1 x 400g tin of chopped tomatoes

mixed dried herbs, or fresh parsley, thyme or rosemary

a squeeze of lemon or 2 tsp bottled lemon juice

a grind of black pepper

This curious soup dating from somewhere in the 1500s is an ideal use for stale, old bread and past-its-best wine. I have tweaked it a little, as my palate isn't quite the same as that of a medieval peasant, but the result is rather lovely. You can use this as a base and add a tin of white beans to thicken it, with herbs; cannellini, haricot or borlotti beans would work nicely, but then so would a tin of cheap baked beans with the tomato sauce rinsed off. Leftovers can be used as a starting point for a casserole or rough Bolognese – just add sausages or mince, an onion or two, and away you go.

1 Toss the onion into a saucepan with a little oil or butter. Tear up the bread into chunks, or slice it if it is really rather stale, and add that, too. Cook on medium heat to soften the onions and gently brown the bread.

2 Add the wine, stock, tomatoes and herbs, and bring to the boil. Reduce to a simmer, stirring, and cook for 20–30 minutes until thickened and glossy.

3 Add the lemon juice and pepper, and serve. A handful of cheese on top wouldn't go amiss, but it is just as fine without.

SPINACH, LENTIL AND LEMON SOUP

SERVES 4–6

200g lentils

2 large onions, finely sliced or diced

1 full bulb of garlic, roughly chopped

1 tbsp cumin seeds

½ tsp mustard seeds

½ tsp chilli flakes, or less to taste

oil or knob of butter, for frying

1 lemon

200g fresh spinach or frozen spinach, allowed to defrost

a fistful of fresh parsley or coriander leaves

600ml vegetable or chicken stock

a pinch of salt and a bit of cracked black pepper

This soup is a variation on one I found in *Saha*, by Greg and Lucy Malouf, many years ago. I lost the book to a good friend, but I remember the basics of this simple, almost store-cupboard recipe, and over the years that followed I made it my own. It is a little fiddly, but completely worth it for its freshness and striking colour. I make it with green lentils, but it works equally well with split yellow peas, red lentils, black-eyed peas, black beans, chickpeas or any other pulse you can think of.

1 First rinse the lentils and pop them into a saucepan that will easily take double their volume. Cover with cold water – do not add any salt at this stage as your lentils may seize and refuse to soften. Bring to the boil and reduce to a simmer, keeping an eye on them.

2 Toss the onions into a new, large pot. Add the garlic, cumin and mustard seeds and chilli flakes with a slosh of oil or a knob of butter. Cook on gentle heat to soften the alliums and coax the spices. Finely chop the lemon, rind and all, and toss it into the pot. Stir occasionally to prevent it from sticking and burning.

3 Stuff the spinach and herbs into a blender with a little water, and pulse well to liquidise. It should be alarmingly green, bold and invigorating. Stand this to one side for a moment, you'll need it in a minute.

4 When the lentils are soft and swollen, drain and rinse them to knock off any residue that has formed on the surface. Tip them in with the onions and garlic. Cover everything with the stock, bring to the boil and reduce to a simmer. Cook for a further 20 minutes or so to soften the lentils – the longer the better.

5 When ready to serve, pour in the bright green liquid from the blender. Stir well, and season to taste. You can eat the chunks of lemon, if you like; they're perfectly edible and the sharp, bitter explosion is a welcome contrast to the deep earthiness of the cumin and lentils. This soup freezes well and it forms an excellent base for a curry, too.

CARROT AND GREEK CHEESE SOUP

SERVES 2

1 onion, sliced

1 tbsp oil

200g carrots

1 potato, diced

1 chicken or vegetable stock cube dissolved in 500ml boiling water

100g natural yoghurt

fistful of coriander (leaves and stalks), plus extra to serve

50g feta or Greek-style cheese, crumbled, to serve

This recipe came about by accident as part of a challenge I set for my readers. Turning the tables, I took a photo of my weekly food shop and asked them for ideas as to what I could make out of it. Towards the end of the week, I had a glut of carrots left, some cheap 'Greek-style cheese' – that's imitation feta from the value range at the supermarket – and some other bits and bobs. And this was the result. (Pictured overleaf.)

1 Toss the onion into a pan with the oil, and sauté on medium heat for 5 minutes to soften.

2 Dice the carrots and add to the pan with the potato. Pour over the stock, bring to the boil, then reduce to a simmer and cook for 20 minutes to soften.

3 Pour the vegetables and stock into a blender, tip in the yoghurt and coriander and blitz until smooth.

4 Pour into bowls, with extra coriander and crumbled cheese to serve.

TIP

● Leftovers can be poured over pasta with extra cheese crumbled on top for a speedy lunch.

SPICED POTATO SOUP WITH CHILLI AND YOGHURT

MAKES 2 DECENT
PORTIONS

**2 large onions,
chopped**

oil, for frying

1 tsp chilli flakes

**2 tsp cumin, seeds
or ground**

1–2 tsp turmeric

**1 x 400g tin of new
potatoes in water**

**a pinch of salt and
a good grind of
black pepper**

**1 chicken or
vegetable stock cube
dissolved in 500ml
boiling water**

200g natural yoghurt

The eagle-eyed among you may notice that this recipe is very similar to a simple potato soup in my first cookbook, *A Girl Called Jack*. And you would be right, because come the winter, or even a snifter of autumn, a hot, thick, carb-loaded warming potato soup is something that is cooked in my kitchen with comforting regularity. I believe you can't have too many good soup recipes under your belt, so please, enjoy the upgraded version as much as I do. (Pictured overleaf.)

1 Toss the onions into a saucepan with a little oil. Cook gently for a few minutes on medium heat to soften, then add the chilli flakes, cumin and turmeric. Stir regularly to prevent them sticking to the pan.

2 Drain and rinse the tinned spuds, slice or dice them, and toss them into the pot. I like to cook them in the oil a little first to inject some flavour into them, as tinned spuds sometimes need a little help in the yum department. Season with a little salt and pepper and cook for a few minutes.

3 Cover with the stock and turn the heat up to get it all boiling. When it comes to a boil, reduce to a vigorous simmer and cook for around 15 minutes. Remove from the heat and tip into a blender, then whizz to a nice smooth soup.

4 To serve, add the yoghurt – DO NOT just dollop it into the pan as it will split, which is perfectly edible in a sour kind of way but does look rather off-putting. Put the yoghurt in a separate bowl, add 2 tablespoons of the soup to it, and stir quickly to combine. Repeat this step about six times, gradually thinning the yoghurt and warming it without it splitting.

5 When the yoghurt-soup mix is warm to touch, tip it into the remaining soup and stir in.

SPICED CAULIFLOWER, BUTTER BEAN AND ALMOND SOUP

SERVES 4,
EASILY FROZEN

200g fresh or frozen cauliflower, diced (about ½ head of cauliflower)

1 onion, finely sliced

2 fat garlic cloves or 3 smaller ones, finely sliced

2 tbsp oil

1 fresh chilli, sliced, or a pinch of chilli flakes

scant 1 tsp cumin, seeds or ground, plus extra to serve

scant ½ tsp turmeric, plus extra to serve

1 x 400g tin of white beans (I use butter beans, but a tin of ordinary baked beans, thoroughly rinsed to get rid of the sticky tomato sauce, is a great cheap substitute)

4 tbsp ground almonds

1 chicken stock cube dissolved in 400ml boiling water, or 400ml water

fresh coriander, to serve (optional, but pretty)

This is a recipe based on a scribbled note I found scrunched up and stuffed in my purse, from a conversation over lunch with my friend Janet, who is excellent with food. The little yellow sticky is around two years old and simply said: 'Janet soup. Cauli, B. bean, almond, pap/spice.' Two years on, here's my interpretation of 'Janet Soup' – probably bearing no resemblance to the original, but absolutely delicious nonetheless. (Pictured on previous page.)

1 Toss the cauliflower into a medium pan along with the onion and garlic. Add the oil, chilli, cumin and turmeric, and fry on medium heat until the onion is softened and the cauli is a nutty brown colour.

2 Drain and rinse the beans, tip into the pan, stir in the ground almonds and pour over the chicken stock or water, and bring to the boil. Boil vigorously for a few minutes to heat through, then reduce to a simmer for around 20 minutes for small white beans and 40 minutes for butter beans. However, as with all legume-based recipes, this benefits from a very long, low slow cook to really break the beans down into a luscious creamy delight.

3 Blitz in the blender until smooth, and heat through to serve. Garnish with an extra shake of cumin and turmeric and a scattering of fresh coriander.

TIP

● If you have any cauliflower left over you could slice it finely and toast it in a dry pan, then serve on top of each bowl of soup.

CHILLED PEA SOUP

SERVES 2

1 tbsp oil

1 smallish potato, diced

4 spring onions, sliced

1 small red chilli, sliced, or a pinch of chilli flakes

1 fat garlic clove, crushed

1 vegetable or chicken stock cube dissolved in 500ml boiling water

250g frozen petits pois

fistful of fresh coriander leaves

1 tsp sugar

1 tbsp lime juice

200g natural yoghurt, or 120ml cream for an indulgent version

Chilled pea and mint soup is everywhere at the moment – I'm a fan of pea and coriander. It's lovely served warm, but I like mine chilled – cool and refreshing, with a little hot chilli surprise. (Pictured on previous page.)

1 Warm the oil in a saucepan and add the potato, spring onions, chilli and garlic (reserve some chopped onion and chilli to garnish, if you like). Cook for 5 minutes on medium heat, stirring occasionally.

2 Pour over the stock, bring to the boil and simmer for 15 minutes until the potato is very tender. Add the peas and cook for no more than 5 more minutes, so they keep their bright, fresh taste and colour.

3 Tip the lot into a blender, add the coriander, sugar, lime juice and yoghurt, and blend until smooth.

4 Pour back into the pan and warm through, or chill for an hour, then serve garnished with the chopped onion and chilli if you like.

TIPS

● Replace the yoghurt with coconut milk for a sweeter flavour.

● Leftovers can be frozen, and make a great base for a Thai-style curry with vegetables or chicken.

● If you need to cool it quickly, serve the soup in a bowl on ice.

SPICED SPLIT PEA AND YOGHURT SOUP (V)

SERVES 4

**100g dried yellow
split peas**

**1 onion, finely
chopped**

**2 garlic cloves, finely
chopped**

2 carrots, sliced

1 tbsp oil

**1 tsp each ground
cumin and turmeric,
or 2 tsp garam
masala**

100g natural yoghurt

**handful of fresh
parsley or coriander
leaves, torn, to
garnish**

This recipe came about after I bought a bag of yellow split peas on a whim to make a daal, and never quite got around to it. Fishing them out of the back of the store-cupboard, I was determined to finally put them to use, so I asked my blog readers what they thought I should make out of them. Several people enthusiastically suggested soup – so with a little trial and error and a lot of surreptitious tasting along the way, here's what I ended up with. Thick, creamy, comforting and delicious – I'll never be at a loss for what to do with a bag of split peas again.

1 Pop the dried yellow split peas into a bowl and cover with water. Cover the bowl with cling film or a plate, and leave to soak for at least 8 hours, or overnight.

2 Add the onion, garlic and carrots to a medium-sized saucepan with the oil and spices, and sauté on medium heat for 5 minutes to soften.

3 Drain and thoroughly rinse the peas, then tip into the pan. Cover with water and stir well. Bring to the boil, then reduce to a simmer. Simmer for 20 minutes, or until the peas and carrots are soft.

4 Pour the mixture into a blender, tip in the yoghurt and pulse until almost smooth. I like to leave mine a bit rough and chunky for a great texture, but it's up to you. Serve hot, with bread to dunk in, and torn parsley or coriander to garnish.

TIPS

● **Vegans – replace the yoghurt with soy yoghurt, or use almond or rice milk for a real treat.**

● **Freeze leftovers in small portions to use as a spicy, chunky pasta sauce or the base for a curry for leftover chicken. Just defrost in a sauté pan with a little water, stir in the chicken and any green veg you have to hand, and you have a pretty instant curry. It works just as well without the chicken, too. I'm thinking green beans, broccoli, peas – a colourful, healthy, sensationally quick dinner.**

GARLIC SOUP

SERVES 2

2 garlic bulbs

1 large onion

1 tbsp oil

a pinch of salt and a bit of cracked black pepper

1 tbsp butter

1 chicken stock cube dissolved in 500ml boiling water

1 tsp chopped fresh thyme or mixed dried herbs

200ml cream

fistful of finely grated hard strong cheese, to serve

a squeeze of lemon juice, to serve

Some readers may be sceptical, or even downright disgusted, at the thought of putting two whole bulbs of garlic in a soup, but slowly cooked, garlic is a beautifully sweet and soft flavour – the long slow roast knocks off the harsh notes of its raw state, and this may well surprise you.

1 Preheat the oven to 180°C/350°F/gas 4.

2 Break the garlic bulbs into cloves, quarter the onion, and toss everything into a roasting dish with the oil and a few pinches of salt and pepper. Cover the roasting dish with foil and cook on the middle shelf for 30 minutes, or until the garlic cloves are soft and tender.

3 Transfer the garlic to a plate or bowl to cool for a few minutes until cool enough to handle. Gently melt the butter in a saucepan and squeeze out the garlic from each clove into the pan. Toss in the onion and stir together. Pour over the chicken stock and add the herbs, bring to the boil and remove from the heat.

4 Pour into a blender with the cream and blitz until smooth. Pour back into the pan and warm through, then serve with hard cheese and a squeeze of lemon.

ROAST CARROT AND CHICKPEA SOUP (VE)

SERVES 4

3 medium carrots, thickly sliced

1 x 400g tin of chickpeas, drained and rinsed (drained weight 240g)

4 fat garlic cloves

2 tbsp oil

1 small or ½ large onion, finely sliced

½ tsp cumin, seeds or ground

a pinch of chilli flakes

800ml weak vegetable stock (½ stock cube will do)

I woke up one cold morning craving carrot soup – it's all rock and roll round here these days. I was a bit snuffly around the edges, sore throat and generally feeling a bit sorry for myself, and limping around tragically on a still-broken left foot. This may be the most self-pitying recipe introduction to date. But basically, I fancied something warm, and sweet, and comforting, and easy to do. Something I could fling into the oven and forget about, and get something good inside. Carrot led to roast carrot, and garlic, and some chickpeas for protein and good measure. The result is a subtly spiced, hearty, sweet and delicious soup. It's like the soup equivalent of a cuddle, this one. And it's suitable for all my lovely vegan readers, too. Hurrah.

1 Preheat the oven to 180°C/350°F/gas 4. Toss the carrots into a roasting tin. Add the chickpeas to the tin with the whole garlic cloves. Pour over the oil and give it all a shuffley-shake to lightly coat it, then pop it in the oven for 20 minutes.

2 When the first 20 minutes is up, remove the roasting tin from the oven, scatter the onion, cumin and chilli over, and give it all another shake. Cook for a further 20 minutes.

3 Remove the garlic cloves from the roasting tin, and tip the rest of the contents into a blender – keeping some chickpeas aside to garnish, if you like that sort of thing. Squeeze in the soft garlic from the cloves (don't put the skins in the blender, they end up like tiny bits of wet tissue that stick to the roof of your mouth. We learn from our errors, round here, and pass the wisdom on – though in my defence that was many years ago). Add the stock and blend until smooth.

4 Remove from the blender and warm through, garnishing with the reserved chickpeas to serve, if you like.

BROCCOLI STALK AND BARLEY SOUP

SERVES 1

1 large broccoli stalk, diced

oil, for frying (optional)

1 chicken stock cube dissolved in 300ml boiling water

30g pearl barley

30g natural yoghurt, to serve

I made this for the annual Live Below The Line challenge, where participants cook on £1 a day to fundraise for their chosen charity that is tackling food poverty. This was the result of a small portion of leftover pearl barley and the stalk of a broccoli head, but you can use rice and the florets instead.

1 Grab a non-stick pan, or a griddle if you have that sort of thing lying around the house. Personally I have one favourite, large, shallow non-stick pan I use for everything; it doesn't get the fancy lines on it that you would get from a cast-iron griddle but having spent some of my errant youth flinging skinless-boneless-tasteless-chicken onto a griddle in a local Harvester, I don't have positive associations with identikit charcoal lines on food anyway. Pop it on the hob and crank up the heat to shit-hot.

2 Fling in the diced broccoli and turn the heat down to medium-low, depending on the size of your burner: big burner low, little burner medium. You want some heat, but not so much – the pan should be hot hot already. Stir the broccoli to disturb it a bit and stop it sticking, as you want a light char rather than something that tastes like you're chewing an ashtray . . . Add a tiny bit of oil if your pan needs it. When it's a bit soft around the edges, remove from the heat and allow to cool a little.

3 Give it a minute or two, then add the stock (adding water then crumbling the cube in is fine, it will all come together in the end) then the pearl barley. Return to the heat and simmer for 20 minutes or until the pearl barley is soft and swollen.

4 To serve, add the yoghurt – DO NOT just dollop it into the pan as it will split, which is perfectly edible in a sour kind of way but does look rather off-putting. Put the yoghurt in a separate bowl, add 2 tablespoons of the soup to it, and stir quickly to combine. Repeat this step about six times, gradually thinning the yoghurt and warming it without it splitting.

5 When the yoghurt-soup mix is warm to touch, tip it into the remaining soup and stir in. And serve. Voilà. Broccoli stalk and barley soup.

ALLIUM SOUP

SERVES 4

700g assorted onions, finely sliced

4 fat garlic cloves, peeled

2 tbsp oil (or butter if you're feeling profligate)

a pinch of salt

a splash of red or white wine

1 litre good-quality stock (vegetable for vegans and vegetarians, but I used chicken myself)

2 tbsp vinegar (red, white or cider all work well to cut through the super sweetness of the onion)

1 tsp mixed herbs, fresh or dried

I consulted my rather large copy of the *Leiths Cookery Bible* for classic onion soup guidance and exclaimed aloud when I read that the onions should be cooked for at least an hour. Pfffffft, I said. 'That's about right ... ' nudged a chef friend with twenty-five years' experience and a few onion soups under her belt. And so, an hour it was. And it was worth it, for soft and succulent sweet onion soup, but if the thought of sweating onions for an hour fills you with dread, they soften beautifully after 20 minutes and you'll still have a pretty good base to work with, just use a little less vinegar ...

I managed to use up half a red onion, a large white one, six straggly spring ones and a contender for the world's smallest shallot, but any old onions will do, even dried-up stragglers and bits and pieces.

1 Toss the onions and whole garlic cloves into a heavy-bottomed saucepan. Add the oil or butter, and salt, and cook on the lowest heat your hob can manage, stirring occasionally until soft and translucent.

2 When your onions are soft soft and delicious, pour over the wine, then stock, then vinegar. Add the herbs, bring to the boil, reduce to a simmer and cook for a further 15–60 minutes, depending on patience, budget, electricity bills, etc. To cheat, boil furiously for a few minutes then remove from the heat and cover with a plate or lid or tin foil and leave to stand for an hour to cool completely, then warm through to serve. The covering retains some of the heat so it carries on cooking, without chewing away at your gas or electricity supplies – it's a trick I love and use often!

3 When ready, serve – I had mine with toast spread thinly with mustard, topped with cheese. Delicious and decadent and just the thing for a chilly winter's evening.

PAPPA AL POMODORO (VE)

2 fat garlic cloves, finely sliced

a pinch of salt

4 tbsp oil (*The River Café Cookbook* uses olive oil, but it's gone the way of the Pugliese in this recipe, i.e. NOT HERE)

1 x 400g tin of chopped tomatoes

1 sprig of fresh rosemary or 1 tsp mixed dried herbs

60g bread, crusts are best but any bread will do (approx 2 slices medium-cut bread)

1 tsp sugar (optional)

I love a good tomato soup, and quite often with the humble tomato, simplicity is key. So imagine my delight, yesterday evening, finding a recipe for Pappa al Pomodoro while idly leafing through the iconic *River Café Cookbook* (Rose Gray and Ruth Rogers). I'd never heard of it, but fell in love instantly – garlic, salt, herbs, tomatoes and a little bread. Of course, the original calls for fresh tomatoes in late summer and 'open-textured white bread made with olive oil, such as Pugliese', given that the River Café is famous for tremendously good Italian cooking (and was home to a fledgling Jamie Oliver, Sam and Sam Clark of Moro and many many other great chefs of our time).

I decided to see if I could make my own version, from my basics, including my stash of old bits of bread. Who has a toddler or fussy teenager, or even adult, in their household that doesn't eat their crusts? I used to battle with my Small Boy in the morning about the crusts on his toast until I gave up. If he doesn't like them, he doesn't like them, and giving his toast a quick trim is easier than ten minutes of parrying – me insisting that he eats them, him nibbling and giving me looks out of the corner of his eye and grimacing and whining. Oh, it's just not worth it, is it? So now I trim them off and fling them in a bag in the freezer. I blitz them into breadcrumbs when I need a small amount of them, rather than waste a whole loaf of bread, but today I dug some out for this soup. Bread crust and tinned tomato soup, given a fancy Italian name. Stay with me, it's utterly delicious . . .

Recipe continues overleaf

1 Add the garlic to a saucepan with the salt. Pour over the oil and turn the heat on very very gently – I do garlic then heat, because quite often I'm doing a gazillion things at once in my kitchen, and the oil gets too hot because I decide to quickly wash something up and the garlic goes in and burns and I have to start the whole thing again. It just needs a gentle soften here, so garlic, salt, oil, gentle heat. Burnt garlic stinks. In all kinds of ways.

2 After a minute, pour over the chopped tomatoes and add 250ml water and all the herbs, and bring to the boil. Stir well, then reduce the heat and simmer for 15 minutes, until the soup thickens and concentrates. It might seem like a lot of water, but trust me, it needs it, and it's going to have even more in a minute ...

3 After 15 minutes, tear up the bread and fling it in. Add 250ml water (if you're sceptical, add it a little at a time, but the bread sucks up a lot of water as it swells from bland boring crusts to soft and soggy pieces of deliciousness). Bring it to the boil again, then cover it to retain as much heat as possible (a lid, a plate, some tin foil) and turn off the heat. Leave it to stand for as long as you can bear it – I managed half an hour before I dived back in, but it's one of those dishes that improves the longer it stands around doing its thing, hanging out on the hob, developing its flavours.

4 Warm through to serve. Depending on your tomatoes, it might be a little sharp, so stir in the sugar as it warms through to adjust it (although it shouldn't be after all that cooking and hanging around, but not all tomatoes are created equal). After me – nom nom nom nom nom nom nom ...

KALE, BARLEY AND CUMIN SOUP (V)

SERVES 4

200g pearl barley

3 small onions, red or white, finely sliced

6 fat garlic cloves, chopped

2 tbsp oil or butter, for frying

1 tsp cumin, seeds or ground

a pinch of salt and a bit of cracked black pepper

2 large carrots

1.5 litres vegetable stock

grated zest and juice of 1 lemon

1 tbsp sugar

½ tsp turmeric

1 tbsp red or white wine vinegar

a good handful of kale, chopped

100g natural yoghurt, to serve (optional)

Barley is one of the cheapest grains currently available in shops and supermarkets. My mum made pearl barley soup for us when I was a child, loaded with tiny chopped spring vegetables: carrots, spring greens and nutty pearl barley. I've taken her Northern Irish heritage and added some of my favourite spices for a warming, wholesome soup. Soaking the barley overnight isn't essential, but it softens it a little, which shortens the cooking time needed. If you forget to soak it, or decide to cook this off the cuff, just add half an hour to the cooking time from when you add the barley.

1 First, rinse the barley, then tip into a bowl and cover with cold water, then cover and leave to soak for an hour or so, ideally overnight. When soaked, drain and rinse it, and set to one side.

2 Toss two of the onions and the garlic into a saucepan with the oil or butter, cumin and a pinch of salt. Cook on very low heat for 20 minutes, stirring occasionally to cook evenly. When the onion and garlic are softened, grate one of the carrots and add to the onions and garlic, and stir. Add the barley, pour over the stock, squeeze in the lemon juice and bring to the boil.

3 Cover the pan and reduce to a simmer for 40 minutes, checking every now and again that there is enough liquid – if the soup starts to dry out, add a cup of water (about 250ml) and stir well.

4 After 30 minutes, start to prepare the garnish. Grate the remaining carrot, and pop into a frying pan with the remaining sliced onion and a little oil. Fry on medium heat until soft. Add the sugar, turmeric and vinegar and crank the heat up high to caramelise, stirring all the time to stop it sticking and burning.

5 To serve, stir through the kale then ladle the soup into bowls and top with yoghurt, spiced carrots and onions, and a pinch of lemon zest. Enjoy.

TIP

● It's much easier to zest a whole lemon rather than one that's been halved and squeezed, so do this first of all.

MINESTRONE (VE)

MAKES 6 MUG-
SIZED PORTIONS
OR 4 GENEROUS
BOWLFULS

1 onion, diced

**2 fat garlic cloves,
chopped**

1 carrot, diced

1 tbsp oil

**1 x 400g tin of
chopped tomatoes**

**1 vegetable stock
cube dissolved in
600ml boiling water**

**100g broken-up pasta
or spaghetti**

**½ tsp mixed dried
herbs**

**100g frozen or fresh
spinach (optional)**

**1 x 400g tin of baked
beans**

I often receive letters and emails from friends, family and readers asking for ideas for cheap lunches. Aside from the ubiquitous cheese sandwich or homemade scone-muffin-type-thing and an apple, banana or pear, one of my favourite staple lunches is A Good Hearty Soup. And nothing says hearty soup quite like one packed with pasta, beans and chunky vegetables!

I've been making minestrone soup for so long, I'm amazed it didn't make it into either of my previous books – but I guess I'd never taken the time to write the recipe down and think about it too much. It's one of my staples for a leftover half tin of beans or chopped tomatoes, a scraggy little carrot or half an onion in the bottom of the veg drawer, tired greens, and those little broken bits of pasta in the bottom of the bag, or odds and sods of pasta that aren't quite enough to do anything with. I keep all the last few bits of pasta, and the broken bits, in a large jar, smashed to smithereens – perfect for tossing into soups like this one. Why buy speciality tiny pasta when you can make your own?!

1 Toss the onion and garlic into a heavy-bottomed saucepan with the carrot and pour over the oil, stir, and cook on medium heat for around 5 minutes to start to soften.

2 When the veg have started to soften, pour over the chopped tomatoes and add the stock. Crank the heat right up, toss in the smashed-up pasta pieces and the mixed dried herbs, and bring it all to the boil. When it's bubbling away, stir it well, add the frozen spinach here, if using (fresh greens go in at the end, otherwise they go limp and greyish and just not very nice, but frozen ones need time to defrost), and reduce to medium heat and simmer for 10 minutes, or until your tiny pieces of pasta are soft and swollen.

3 Meanwhile, thoroughly rinse the baked beans, tip into the pan and stir through. If you're using fresh greens, chop them up into little pieces and stir them through to serve.

4 And voilà – minestrone. Comforting, carby, beany goodness, perfect for popping into a jar or a flask to take to work. This soup freezes well, and actually improves in the freezer, so take one portion to work with you (or have it at home, if you're a homebody), and save the rest for later – and congratulate yourself on your hot, cheap lunch date. Hurrah!

TIP

● I'm often asked why I don't heat the oil first, like many other cooks and chefs do, and it's because even after all this time I'm not very fast at the whole vegetable-chopping-up malarkey, and so the oil gets too hot and it sizzles and burns the veg and it all just doesn't work for me that way round. So I do all the chopping, and then add it all to the pan and heat it through. If you are a super-fast and fancy chopper, you might want to heat the oil first and save yourself a minute or two.

A PACKET OF PASTA OR A BAG OF RICE

Carbs are an eternal staple in my cupboard – I keep three kinds of pasta on the go at all times, and thanks to good friends knowing how obsessed I am with it, I currently have an array of jars of all beautiful whirls and swirls of the stuff. Really, though, you can make any of these recipes with the basic value-range penne or spaghetti – my general rule is thinner sauces with spaghetti and chunkier kinds with penne, but my Italian readers may be slightly horrified at that. Those of you with a sensitive disposition re the rules of food may want to look away now as I say that I have only ever made two risottos in my life with Arborio risotto rice; one was for Mary Portas and Sue Perkins, so it had to be pretty special, and the other was in a professional kitchen. I use long grain rice for my risottos, the same as my mother did, and with a little stirring and tender care, they can be just as soft, just as creamy, just as delicious as the stuff that costs four times as much.

MUG MARMITE MAC AND CHEESE

SERVES 1

75g macaroni or other short pasta

2 tsp butter

½ tsp Marmite or other yeast extract

20g hard strong cheese (you might want to use more, but I like hard and strong and scant myself)

Friends know that my Marmite obsession is almost as out of control as my peanut butter obsession. In leaner times, I would substitute Marmite, which was well out of my budget range, with a paste made from a crumbled value-range beef stock cube, mixed with boiling water and allowed to cool. Smeared onto toast with butter, it delivered that tongue-warming tingle and salty kick I used to get from my yeast-extract friend. These days, my cupboard has a jar of Marmite in it for toast and snacks, and today it went in here, too. If you're a hater, not a lover, just leave it out – or, of course, you could always cook your pasta in a stock made from a crumbled cube and we'll call it quits …

1 Tip the pasta into a mug and cover with 250ml cold water (you can also crumble in ½ beef stock cube – don't knock it 'til you've tried it). Cover the mug with cling film and pierce it several times, or balance a small saucer on top – make sure neither mug nor saucer have any metal on, please, the Fire Service are busy enough.

2 Stand the mug in a bowl or jug – you'll see why in a sec. Cook on full power for 2 minutes, then remove the mug. It's usual for water to bubble up over the sides and drench the bottom of your microwave, so to save cleaning it up and topping it up again, which will slow your cooking time down, just tip the water back into the mug.

3 Give it all a good stir and leave to stand for a minute. Repeat this step twice more, until your pasta is soft and swollen. You may need to add a splash more water here or there, which is fine – not all microwaves, nor pasta, are created equal.

4 Add the butter, stir in the Marmite and grate over the cheese. Cook for 1 more minute on full power, stir well and serve.

TIP

● For a portable version, mix together oil, instead of butter, with the Marmite and finely grated hard cheese and pop the paste into a small container. Separately measure a portion of the pasta and take both containers with you to wherever you're off to that has a microwave. Now all you need is to cook the pasta as instructed, stir in the paste, and voilà.

CARROT RIBBON PASTA

SERVES 1

75g spaghetti

a handful of fresh herbs

2 tbsp lemon juice, fresh or bottled

30ml oil (I used sunflower)

a good pinch of salt and a bit of cracked black pepper

1 carrot

2 tbsp breadcrumbs or grated hard strong cheese

This recipe has been adapted for the microwave from one of my favourite, simple ones from my first cookbook, *A Girl Called Jack*. Originally born of a way to use up a bulk-buy bag of carrots (in the days before the guinea pig!), and to make veg exciting for a then two-year-old boy, it's still a bright staple in my home today. It's beautiful, simple and delightful and can be enjoyed all year round. Use whatever herbs you have to hand for the green sauce – I usually like basil or parsley in this one.

The breadcrumbs on top can be swapped for hard strong cheese, for my non-vegan readers, and leave out the pinch of salt – although I hear rumour that vegan cheeses are available quite widely these days ...

1 First grab a bowl that's microwave-safe and doesn't have any metal embellishments on (sorry to nag, but you might be new around here).

2 Break the spaghetti in half so it fits in the bowl, and place it in the bottom. Cover it with cold water, half-filling the bowl. Pop a plate on top, or cover with cling film, and pierce a couple of holes in it with a sharp knife (the cling film, that is, not the plate). Cook on full power for 2½ minutes. Stir and leave to stand for a minute. Cook on full power for another 2½ minutes. Stir and leave to stand for a minute. It should be just cooked, but not all microwaves nor spaghetti are created equal, so if it is unpleasantly crunchy, give it another 2 minutes – but you don't want it flobby and sticky, because it will have another minute yet.

3 While the microwave is doing its thing, make the green dressing for your pasta. Finely chop the herbs (I put mine into a teacup and attack them with scissors, containing them all in one place. It's pretty satisfying, too). Add the lemon juice, oil and salt and stir well. Stand to one side. (The dressing, not you.)

4 To make the carrot ribbons, use a vegetable peeler to strip the carrot into long, thin ribbons, then stack them up and slice them carefully into thinner pieces. Or you can grate them, that's cool, too. Pop the carrot ribbons in with the pasta for a last minute of cooking, then drain and toss in the green sauce. Top with breadcrumbs or the grated cheese, a grind of pepper, and serve. Voilà.

TIPS

• You can either whizz some bread in a food processor to make breadcrumbs, or collect old bits of bread as you go along. I smash up the crusts I cut off for my son, and the ends of the loaf, the stale badly wrapped piteous pittas, etc, and store them in a jar next to the bread bin with a teaspoon of salt shaken through to keep them dry, for things like this.

• For a portable lunch, you can make the whole thing in advance and pop it into a jar or container and take it with you, reheating it in the microwave, if you like – but it's yummy cold, too. The dressing stops the pasta from clumping together when it's cold, although it might need a quick ping to bring it to room temperature. Or make the dressing and ribbon the carrots, and combine the two in one container. Pop the pasta in another container and cook it at lunchtime, then toss the carrots/sauce/crumbs through.

• And if you're feeling super healthy, try it with wholemeal pasta and add some ribboned courgettes, too. And sultanas. And basically do what you like. Veg is fun, kids. At least, that's what I tell mine. Happy eating!

PARSNIP MAC AND CHEESE (V)

SERVES 2, EASILY
DOUBLED, TRIPLED,
ETC

**1 tbsp any kind of
flour**

**2 tbsp oil, butter or
butter-ish spread**

**80g strong cheese,
grated**

300ml milk

**1 decent-sized
parsnip, or
2 tiddlers**

**¼ tsp dried
rosemary, thyme
or mixed herbs
(optional)**

**a pinch of salt and a
bit of cracked black
pepper**

**160g macaroni or
other short pasta**

This recipe came from both a love of parsnips and a need to smuggle vegetables into Small Boy who, when aged six, started to rebel against anything clearly identifiable as 'from the ground'. I received similar messages from parents with alarming regularity, asking how to sneak veg into their beloveds' dinners without causing a high drama, and so I set to work. This was such a hit with my small one that I confessed to the parsnips at the end, when he had scraped his bowl clean.
I often double the recipe and freeze it in portions, in recycled jars or plastic containers, for an easy night somewhere in the future. If you are freezing in jars, don't fill to the top, as it will expand when frozen, and a freezer full of broken glass is no fun at all. I alternate between rosemary, thyme and cheap mixed dried herbs when making this, but it also marries well with a pinch of nutmeg or a bay leaf or two, or even a little ground cumin if you have it kicking about and are feeling experimental.

1 Make a rough paste to form the base of your sauce, by dolloping the flour and oil or butter into a saucepan – off the heat – and mixing well with a fork to combine. Add the cheese, then pop onto the hob on low heat, stirring to combine as the cheese starts to melt.

2 Add a dash of milk and beat in quickly, then repeat, and repeat, until all of the milk is incorporated. Don't rush this step, as you may end up with a milky sauce with clods of floury dough swimming on top. If this happens, it's not the end of the world. Either fling it into a blender and pulse briefly to combine it, or strain it through a sieve (or tea strainer) to get rid of the lumps, pushing them through with a spoon and stirring well.

3 Grate the parsnip into the pan, add the herbs, if using, and stir well. Cook on low heat, stirring occasionally, for around 15 minutes to thicken. Season with a little salt and pepper to taste.

4 In the meantime, bring a pan of water to boil and drop in the pasta. Cook according to the packet instructions – usually 8–10 minutes for dried pasta – and drain. Toss in the cheesy parsnip sauce and serve.

TIPS

● To make it extra special, tip the pasta and sauce into an ovenproof dish, top with breadcrumbs, and bake at 180°C/350°F/gas 4 for around 10 minutes before serving.

● There is a speedy, heretics' version of this recipe, should you desire it. As with most shortcuts it is not quite as good as the version to which you give care and attention, but I of all people know that sometimes there's a child clinging to your leg or zero shucks to give and standing over a stove is the last thing on your mind. You can just grate the parsnip and cheese and toss into a blender with the flour, butter and milk, season, and tip into a pan with the pasta. Cook it all together, adding a little water, stock or more milk, if required, until the pasta is cooked through. Tip into bowls, add a smattering more cheese, and demolish.

SPAGHETTI ALLA PUTTANESCA

SERVES 2

4 fat garlic cloves

1 fresh red chilli, chopped

2 tbsp oil

1 x 400g tin of chopped tomatoes

1 x 90g tin of sardines in oil, drained but reserve the oil

1 tbsp capers

1 tbsp olives, pitted and diced

a pinch of salt

200g spaghetti

My take on spaghetti alla puttanesca is a little different – I prefer tinned sardines to the more traditional anchovies, and I like to add some of the preserved oil for a distinctive flavour. This dish is a hot, fast joyride for your tastebuds, with its fiery chilli, soft chunks of fish, vinegary capers and salty aftertaste.

1 Roughly chop the garlic – I like mine chunky in a dish like this, but if a mouthful of slightly crunchy garlic will put you off, chop it finely. Put it into a large saucepan with the chilli and oil and sauté on low heat for 2–3 minutes or until the garlic has softened.

2 Pour over the chopped tomatoes and the oil from the sardines, and turn up the heat to bring it to the boil.

3 Carefully remove the bones from the sardines by splitting them, belly and back, with a small, sharp knife. Use the tip of the knife to pick out the large bone in the middle and any others that are visible. Break the sardines into chunks and stir into the sauce. Simmer and let it thicken, then stir through the capers, olives and pinch of salt.

4 Meanwhile, cook the spaghetti according to the packet instructions, usually simmering for 8–10 minutes, and transfer it to the sauce for the last minute or two to finish and coat. Divide between two bowls.

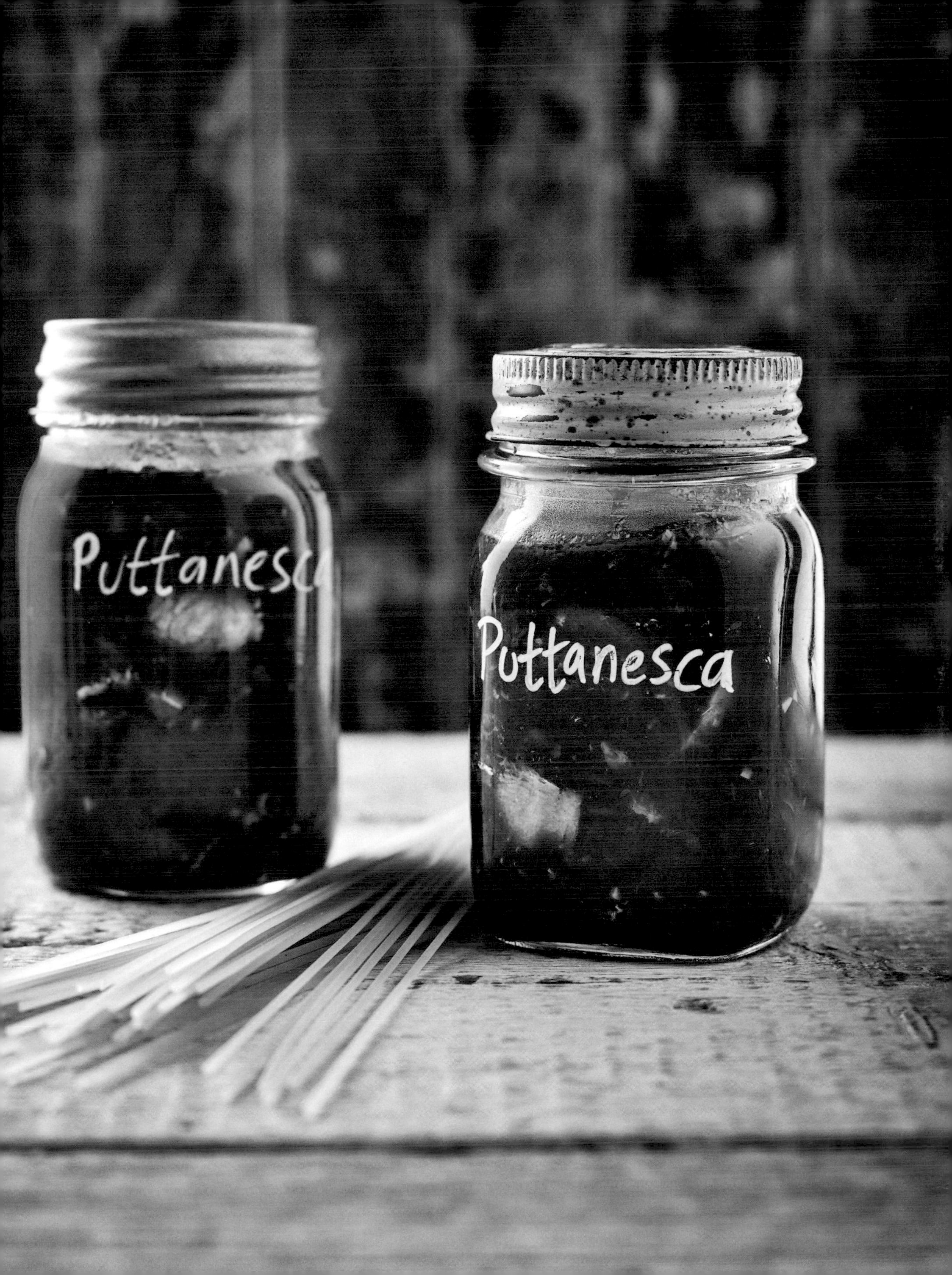

ROASTED CABBAGE PASTA WITH CHEESE (V)

SERVES 2

¼ Savoy cabbage, cut in half

2 tbsp oil

a pinch of salt and a bit of cracked black pepper

150g pasta (I like spaghetti in this one, but any pasta will do)

50g feta or Greek-style cheese

good oil, for drizzling

a pinch of chilli flakes, to serve

I first had roasted cabbage on a very rare holiday to Los Angeles, so long ago now that the sunshine seems like a distant memory. I kept a diary of all the wonderful fresh foods and glorious flavours I enjoyed, making notes to try to transpose them back into something relatable, and easy to replicate, at home. The charred edges of the roasted cabbage were served at the time with a creamy Caesar dressing and paper-thin pieces of hard, stinking cheese, generously garnished with chilli. I admit I was initially unimpressed, remarking sceptically to my travelling partner that they had literally brought us a burnt cabbage. Well, I ate my words along with that 'literally burnt cabbage', as it was a delight.

I have little place for fancy starters in my day-to-day life, but I do love a steaming bowl of pasta on a near-daily basis, so this was born.

1 Preheat the oven to 200°C/400°F/gas 6.

2 Place the cabbage pieces on a baking tray, drizzle over the oil along with the salt and pepper, and cook in the centre of the oven for 10 minutes. Reduce the heat to 180°C/350°F/gas 4 and cook for 15 minutes more. If you get distracted easily or think that sounds like too much fannying around, sling it on 190°C/375°F/gas 5 throughout.

3 Meanwhile, bring a pan of water to the boil, lightly salt it and pop the pasta in. Reduce to a simmer and cook according to the packet instructions, usually 8–10 minutes.

4 When the cabbage is cooked, the edges should be flecked with brown but a fork inserted into the middle should not meet with any significant resistance. Remove from the oven and carefully slice it thinly.

5 Drain the pasta and toss with the sliced cabbage. Crumble in the cheese and toss again to slightly melt it and distribute it evenly. Serve and drizzle a little of your best oil on it to lubricate it, and finish with a pinch of chilli flakes.

LAZARUS PESTO

MAKES 2 DECENT-SIZED JARS

½ **bunch of mint (50g approx)**

½ **bunch of basil (50g approx)**

½ **bunch of parsley (50g approx)**

4 garlic cloves

100g cashew nuts

zest and juice of 1 lemon

50g hard strong cheese, grated

100ml oil (I used groundnut, but vegetable or sunflower would work well)

cooked pasta of your choice, to serve

This came about when I had a large black bunch of mint in the fridge, some sticky soggy parsley and a clump of basil that had seen better days. Add to that a hard rind of cheese and you can see why everyone wants to come to lunch here. I decided to whack it all in the blender and see if I could raise those sad soggy herbs from the dead … And voilà. Lazarus pesto was born, and the guinea pig sulked a little, because he normally gets the ropey dead stuff.

1 Stuff the herbs in the blender – stalks and all – and pulse them to chop them finely. If you don't have a blender, my favourite method of chopping herbs is to pop them into a cup and go at them with kitchen scissors – far tidier and easier than fiddling about with a knife!

2 Finely chop the garlic and nuts (by hand or in the blender), then add to the leaves with the lemon zest and cheese.

3 Squeeze over the lemon juice and pour over the oil, then mix well to make your pesto. If you like it a little looser, add a splash more oil, or water.

4 Serve with cooked pasta of your choice or spoon into clean jars, and top with a thin layer of oil to keep the air out. Pop lids on, and store in the fridge for up to 3 weeks.

SAUSAGNE (SOH-SAN-YAH)

SERVES 6ISH (HA HA HA HA)

1 x 500g box of lasagne sheets

300g sausages (vegetarian or ordinary, depends what floats your sausageboat – cheaper sausages chop more finely)

2 x 400g tins of chopped tomatoes

½ tsp mixed dried herbs – oregano or thyme, or something like it

a pinch of salt and a bit of cracked black pepper

2 mozzarella balls

strong cheese, to taste (not essential, but so good)

some breadcrumbs, to taste (optional)

Making lasagne is an arse. A labour of love. An every-pan atrocity strewn around the desolate wasteland of what was formerly your kitchen. I have made dozens of lasagnes in my short lifetime, and halfway through every single one comes the moment, without fail, whereby I survey the three pans on the hob, the piles of everything, the crap strewn across every available worksurface and some of the not-available ones, too, and I wail inside that I could have just bought one for less than a quid at the supermarket.

One night, craving lasagne but not the work that went with it, I threw this together, and the Sausagne was born. I'm not suggesting for a minute that it is an exact substitute but, my, it ticks all the soft, cheesy, comforting, gooey boxes, and with far less washing up.

1 Preheat the oven to 180°C/350°F/gas 4 and locate a dish suitable for making a lasagne in. Use something deep and absolutely not round – I tried to make a round lasagne once and it was one of the worst ideas I had ever had, and that's saying something.

2 Grab a large mixing bowl. Finely slice the sausages and sling them in. Pour in the chopped tomatoes, add the herbs, a pinch of salt and a bit of pepper and mix it all up together.

3 Spread a layer of sausage-tomato mix into the dish. Layer lasagne sheets on top. Repeat until the sausage mix runs out. It needs to be a little sloppy, as the wetness of the tomatoes is what cooks the lasagne sheets.

4 Place the last lasagne sheets on top. Slice the mozzarella and cover the sheets. Grate some strong cheese on top, sprinkle on some breadcrumbs, if you want them, and bake in the oven for 30 minutes or until golden and gorgeous. And enjoy the sausagne revelation. Lasagne will never be the same again.

CREAMY CANNELLINI AND FENNEL PASTA (VE)

SERVES 4

1 large onion
(about 200g),
finely sliced

2–4 fat garlic cloves
(depending on how
much of a fan you
are), minced or finely
chopped

2 tbsp oil

a pinch of salt

¼ tsp fennel seeds

1 x 400g tin of
cannellini beans,
drained and rinsed
(240g drained weight)

2 tbsp lemon juice

a few sprigs of
parsley or herb of
your choice, to finish

cooked pasta of your
choice, to serve

This pasta dish is packed with protein, but also a very good healthy substitute for cream-packed pasta dishes. As with all bean-based dishes, they benefit from a long, slow cook, so the more time you have to give this, the better the results.

1 Pop the onion and garlic into a large saucepan with the oil. Bring to gentle heat, add a pinch of salt and the fennel seeds and stir lovingly. There's a lot of love going into this dish along the way, it's got the subtle soothing nature of a risotto, so clear the decks and use it as a de-stressor while you stand and stir.

2 Toss the cannellini beans into the pan, squeeze the lemon juice over the top, and cook on low heat for 10 minutes to soften the onions.

3 Add 200ml cold water, then turn up the heat and bring to a boil. Reduce to a simmer, stir, and leave to cook for another 10 minutes. The cannellinis should start to break down and self-purée, thickening the sauce. Stir well and gradually add another 200ml water (you might not need all of it) until most of the beans have broken down and you're left with a soft, creamy, sweet, garlicky, comforting gorgeous sauce. Stir through the herbs.

4 Stir through your pasta, or allow to cool, spoon into jars, label and pop in the fridge until dinner time. I'm putting one in the fridge and one in the freezer for a freebie dinner later in the week.

TIP

● Fennel seeds are not essential if they aren't the sort of thing you have lying around but I'm a Big Fan of them – as a store-cupboard spice, a couple of little fennel seeds go a long, long way.

PUMPKIN AND BACON CARBONARA

SERVES 2

4 fat garlic cloves, finely chopped

20g butter

100g bacon, chopped

1 sprig of rosemary

160g spaghetti

100ml white wine (or Martini would be achingly delicious in this, I just didn't have any)

4 egg yolks

100g pumpkin purée (from a tin or a carved pumpkin)

100ml cream

a fistful of spinach leaves (optional)

50g hard strong cheese, to serve

a generous grinding of black pepper

This is an ideal 'use-up' for the carved innards of a Jack o' Lantern come 1 November, or it's just as easily made with canned pumpkin purée. Vegetarians can omit the bacon, and add a smattering of paprika for a similar smoky taste, instead.

1 Lob the garlic into a pan with the butter on low, barely-there heat to soften and sweeten. (Or peel them and leave them whole for a soft, garlicky treat, if you like that sort of thing.) Toss in the bacon. Strip the rosemary leaves from the stalk, finely chop them (large woody bits of rosemary between your teeth are fairly unpleasant) and toss those in too. Give it all a good stir, and cook gently for 10 minutes to soften the garlic and crisp the bacon.

2 Bring a pan of water to the boil, add the spaghetti and cook according to the packet instructions, usually for 8–10 minutes. Now get your shit together, the next bit happens quickly!

3 Pour the wine over the garlic-bacon-rosemary and crank the heat up to medium–high. In a separate bowl, beat together the egg yolks, pumpkin purée and cream until well combined. Add half a ladle (or a few tablespoons) of the hot pasta cooking water to the egg-pumpkin-cream and mix well. Remove the garlic-bacon-rosemary pan from the heat and slowly add the sauce, stirring well to stop it from splitting. Return the pan to low heat to cook the egg yolks through – don't worry if your sauce looks thin, it will thicken as it cooks.

4 To serve, toss the cooked spaghetti in the creamy sauce, and drop in a handful or two of spinach, if using. Grate over a generous amount of hard strong cheese – mature cheddar, Parmesan, or my old favourite, imitation Parmesan that packs a strong salty punch, and a good grind of black pepper, and enjoy.

TIP

● If the sauce does split with enthusiastic heating, all is not lost! Put it to one side, and make a quick roux with a knob of butter and 1 rounded teaspoon of plain flour in a pan over low heat. Add a splash of water or milk and mix to make a rough paste. Add a splash of the carbonara sauce, stir until smooth, and repeat until all of the sauce is incorporated. Rescued!

CHICKEN LIVER BOLOGNESE

SERVES 4

250g chicken livers

100ml whole milk, for soaking

4 fat garlic cloves, minced

1 large onion, finely sliced

2 tbsp oil or a little butter, plus extra for frying

a pinch of salt

1 tbsp red or white wine vinegar

1 x 400g tin of chopped tomatoes

1 tsp mixed dried herbs, or 1 tsp chopped fresh thyme or oregano

300g spaghetti

Chicken liver is one of those foods I detested throughout my childhood, knowing it only in its school-dinner incarnation: cooked until grey and grainy, with flabby onions and barely a smudge of gravy. When I started writing budget recipes on my blog a few years ago, many readers got in touch to extol the virtues of chicken liver. At around 50p for a large dose of protein, I decided to brave it. This is a much-simplified version of a Bolognese, but the chicken livers need little else. I've learned to avoid school-dinner liver by either cooking it for less than a minute or slowly casseroling it for at least 40 minutes – anything in between seems terrifying.

1 Tip the livers into a colander or sieve and give them a quick blast under the cold tap to clean off any excess blood. Using a small, sharp knife, remove any overly stringy bits and slice the livers fairly thinly. Put them in a bowl, cover with milk and stand to one side to soak. (The milk will be bloody and liver-y afterwards. I wasn't sure what to do with it, so I warmed it through and gave it to the cat, who devoured it. Any other answers on a postcard.)

2 Put the garlic and onion in a large, shallow saucepan or frying pan. Add the oil or butter and salt, and cook on low, slow heat for a few minutes, until starting to soften. Pour over the vinegar, add the tomatoes and herbs, turn up the heat and bring to the boil. Once boiling, reduce to low again for at least 20 minutes and up to an hour, stirring to stop it from sticking as it thickens.

3 The longer you leave it, the better, thicker and glossier it gets. When your sauce is almost ready, put a second pan of water on to boil for the spaghetti. Cook according to the packet instructions, usually simmering for 8–10 minutes.

4 Heat a little oil in a small frying pan. Flash-fry the livers for 20 seconds on each side, then remove from the heat. Tip into the tomato sauce and stir through over low heat.

5 Drain the spaghetti and serve the liver Bolognese on top of the pasta.

MARROW GRATIN

SERVES 4

1 large onion, diced

500g marrow, peeled and diced

2 tbsp oil

1 x 400g tin of chopped tomatoes

200g orzo

a few sprigs of fresh basil, finely chopped

a few sprigs of fresh parsley, finely chopped

1 chicken or vegetable stock cube dissolved in 200ml boiling water

a pinch of salt and a bit of cracked black pepper

1 slice of bread, blitzed into breadcrumbs

100g halloumi, finely grated

Every Sunday in my childhood, my parents, brother and whatever assortment of foster children were living with us at the time, would sit down in the middle of the afternoon to enjoy a proper roast dinner. More often than not it was chicken, usually accompanied by potatoes, greens, carrots and gravy. And then, somewhere in the autumn, everything would get shoved along to make room for a large dollop of my dad's marrow, softened with onion in oil (Dad specifies olive, I defiantly use sunflower) and seasoning. I've enjoyed it over the years as a side, but now I've made it into a gratin for a more substantial dish. He is cross with me for tinkering with it, but I've mollified him by paying homage to his Greek roots with orzo and halloumi in the mix. I think he loves it really.

1 Heat the oven to 200°C/400°F/gas 6. Put the onion into a medium pan with the marrow. Drizzle over the oil and cook on medium heat for a few minutes until the marrow starts to brown around the edges. Pour over the chopped tomatoes and cook for at least 15 minutes.

2 Add the orzo, most of the herbs and the stock, stir, and bring to the boil. Add a pinch of salt and a grind of pepper and cook for a further 8–10 minutes, until the orzo is al dente (it will be finished in the oven). You may need to add a little more water to stop it drying out.

3 Mix the breadcrumbs with the halloumi and remaining herbs. Scatter on top of the marrow mixture. Cook in the oven for 15 minutes until lightly toasted on top. Allow to cool slightly before serving.

CREAMY CRABBY PASTA

SERVES 2

140g pasta (works well with penne and spaghetti but any will do)

½ onion, finely sliced

1 small red chilli, very finely chopped

1 bunch of flat-leaf parsley, very finely chopped, plus extra to serve

1 tbsp lemon juice, plus extra to serve (optional)

oil, for frying

100g natural yoghurt

1 x 75g jar of crab paste (or fish paste)

Eagle-eyed readers may recognise elements of this from my first book *A Girl Called Jack*. The recipe is so popular that I have included it here too, and updated with a new ingredient: crab.

This speedy pasta recipe takes just a few lazy minutes to put together, and tastes absolutely divine. The sharpness of the lemon brings out the crab flavour in the paste, and the yoghurt lends a creamy subtlety.

Top-end restaurants often feature 'creamy salmon mousse' on their menus, which is where I took my inspiration from – except instead of expensive cream I used natural yoghurt, and instead of pulverising a perfectly good piece of salmon or crab flesh, I bought it in a jar, with the hard work already done for me.

I could go on and on about this; I didn't expect to be able to make a restaurant-quality dish from a jar of value-range fish paste, and almost daily I am contacted by readers who have tried this for themselves and been very pleased with the results.

1 Bring some water to the boil in a medium saucepan, and cook the pasta according to the packet instructions, usually simmering for 8–10 minutes.

2 Add the onion, chilli and parsley to a frying pan with the lemon juice and oil, and cook on medium heat to soften the onion.

3 When the pasta is cooked, remove from the heat and drain. Quickly stir the yoghurt and fish paste into the onions to warm through.

4 Tip the pasta into the pan, coat with the sauce, and serve. Garnish with extra parsley and lemon juice, if desired.

SMOKED MACKEREL KEDGEREE

SERVES 2

1 onion, finely sliced

1 tsp cumin, seeds or ground

1 tbsp oil

150g rice

2 eggs

150g smoked mackerel fillets

50g frozen spinach, allowed to defrost

1 tsp turmeric

fresh parsley or coriander, to serve (optional)

This kedgeree was another recipe idea suggested by my readers based on my food shop – and it was an absolute hit. Thank you everyone who suggested it! The mackerel can be replaced with any smoked or strong fish, and the spices can be swapped out for garam masala or curry powder – whatever you have to hand. The onions lend a soft sweetness, the rice fills you up, and the little chunks of egg and mackerel are groan-inducingly gorgeous. Try it. I hereby proclaim this one of my favourite-ever recipes.

1 Add the onion and cumin to a medium sauté or non-stick saucepan with the oil and cook for 5 minutes on medium heat to soften.

2 Add the rice and enough water to cover, and stir. Cook for 15 minutes, until the rice is soft and swollen.

3 Meanwhile, boil a separate small saucepan of water and pop the eggs in. Simmer for 5 minutes to hard-boil, then remove and allow to cool.

4 Flake the mackerel with a fork, peeling back the skin from the fillet (my friend Klein says the skin is delicious fried and eaten like crisps, but I've never found out for myself, as my cat sits at my feet giving me begging eyes whenever there's a scrap of fish to be had!) and add to the pan with the spinach and turmeric. Peel the boiled eggs and slice in half with a sharp knife, then scoop out in chunks and scatter over the finished dish.

5 Serve with fresh parsley or coriander to garnish, if you have it. I didn't – so used the spinach. A green leaf is a green leaf as far as I'm concerned!

GREEN RICE (VE)

SERVES 4

300g rice (I use long grain but you can use any)

a few pinches of salt

300g fresh spinach, or frozen spinach, allowed to defrost

a handful of fresh coriander or parsley

1 garlic clove

2 tbsp lemon juice, fresh or bottled, to finish

This recipe was inspired by the green rice I had at Wahaca, the restaurant chain set up by the dear Thomasina Miers, *Masterchef* winner and beautiful soul. This recipe is admittedly nowhere near as slick as hers, but it was inspired by it, and brings a jewel-like joy to my dining table, time and again.

1 First tip the rice into a sieve and rinse it under a cold running tap to chase away any excess starch. Bring 600ml water to the boil with a little salt, and add the rice. Reduce the heat to medium and gently cook the rice for 15–18 minutes depending on the packet instructions, stirring occasionally to stop it sticking to the pan.

2 When the rice is almost cooked, pop the spinach, 200ml water, coriander or parsley and garlic in a blender and pulse until smooth. Tip this gloriously green mixture into the rice pan and stir it through. Cook for a few minutes more, then stir through the lemon juice and serve.

MICROWAVE COURGETTE, TOMATO AND CHEESE BAKE

SERVES 1

75g rice

½ courgette

1 small garlic clove, minced (see Tip)

100g chopped tomatoes

½ vegetable stock cube (or chicken if you aren't a vegetarian for a sweeter flavour)

a pinch of something green, to finish (optional; I used parsley, but basil, coriander, thyme, rosemary, or even leftover chopped spinach is yummy)

10g hard strong cheese, grated

This recipe from my microwave series is based on a recipe from my book, *A Girl Called Jack*, that I see popping up on my Twitter feed and Facebook pages time and time again – it seems to be a definite favourite among my lovely readers! And so I wondered if it was possible to make a portable microwave version – either for busy evenings, energy-saving cooking, or even to pop into a jar in your work bag to stave off the boredom of yet another soggy cheese sandwich or expensive take-away lunch.

The microwave version has fewer ingredients than the original, oven-baked recipe because I'm trying to keep it simple. I'll also confess that I've made it with a few different rices as an experiment; although the simple, basic, 45p-a-kilo white rice will always be my go-to budget staple, this dish IS delicious with nutty brown rice, too. If it's the kind of thing you keep in the cupboard, use it; if not, don't worry about it.

1 Add the rice to a microwave-safe mixing bowl. Very finely chop the courgette (see Tip) – you want teeny tiny pieces of courgette for this – and add to the bowl. Add the minced garlic clove to the courgette, then pour over the chopped tomatoes and 200ml water and crumble in the ½ stock cube. Stir it all really well, then cover with a saucer or some cling film. If you're using cling film, pierce it with a couple of small holes. If you're using a saucer, don't try to make holes in it.

2 Cook on full power for 3 minutes, then leave to stand for 1 minute. Stir well and repeat: full power for 3 minutes, stand for 1. The rice should be cooked through, but not all rice is created equal (nor microwaves, for that matter) so if it's not quite soft and fluffy, repeat once more.

3 Tip into your eating receptacle of choice (mine is a mug), top with greens and cheese, then ping in the microwave for 30 seconds more just to get the cheese all melty and a bit 'grilled', and devour.

TIPS

● Finely chopping courgette can be a challenge. I did mine with a julienne peeler that my gorgeous friend Rena gave me as a present; it's great for finely chopping vegetables but it bites, and I bear many many tiny cuts on my fingers from this vicious little monkey. You can use an ordinary vegetable peeler to cut your courgette into ribbons, then stack them and finely slice them for the same effect, probably saving the skin on your fingers, too.

● If the thought of chopping one pesky clove of garlic makes your eyes roll to the back of your head, you can ping it in the microwave in its skin for three 10-second bursts, then squeeze the cooked garlic pulp out. Good to know, not so good if your microwave is in a corner of an office full of people who may not appreciate the garlic fumes wafting their way from the microwave vents.

● Dishes like this are an ideal place to smuggle the stalks of fresh herbs, very finely chopped, they have bags of flavour so don't automatically throw them away!

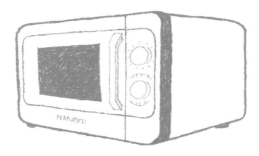

CHILLAF (MICROWAVE CHILLI) (V)

SERVES 1

¼ smallish onion, finely chopped

1 small garlic clove (makes a change from me stipulating a fat one but the small ones have to go in something), finely chopped

½ vegetable stock cube

70g rice (about an espresso cup-sized)

¼ tsp ground cumin

½ tsp paprika (sweet or smoked, depends on preference and store-cupboard)

1 x 200g tin of chopped tomatoes

130g tinned kidney beans (½ x 400g tin, drained and rinsed)

2 squares of dark chocolate, roughly chopped

a splash of vinegar (malt will do)

pinch of salt

100ml natural yoghurt, to serve (optional)

One thing I've noticed from microwave cooking is that flavours change – it's not as simple as flinging a recipe that I would normally cook on the hob into the microwave. Garlic retains a tang of its raw taste if not cut up really finely, as does onion. Spices don't have a long development and infusion time, so some need a little more time, and some need less. Cumin seeds are basically a no, as they stay hard and crunchy with the short ping time, as opposed to a long softening in a pan. Microwave dishes retain a lot more moisture than a pan, so rice needs far less liquid to cook in.

So I had to cook this twice; the first time without rice and by chucking all the ingredients in at the same time. It was delicious, but there was a very slight tang of raw garlic. When I cook chilli on the hob, and indeed lots of other recipes, I'd start by gently sautéeing the garlic and onion to soften it first, then adding the other ingredients. So, I tried again, gently cooking the garlic and onion on low in the microwave first to soften them, the same way I would when cooking on the hob. Seeing I was making it again, I decided to add rice to my chilli to make it a true one-pot meal, and thus the chillaf was born. You can choose to throw all the ingredients in together if you like, but you might like to leave the garlic out, unless you don't mind it super strong.

So with no further ado, here's my microwave chilli pilaf – the chocolate lovers among you will be pleased to note it's got extra chocolate in!

Recipe continues overleaf

1 Pop the onion and garlic into your vessel of choice – I cooked mine in a jug and it worked really well, but think a Tupperware or a bowl would work too. Remember: no metal – metal in microwaves sets fire to things, even the smallest amount of metal embellishment on a plate could be disastrous.

2 Add 1 tablespoon of water to stop them from sticking, cover with cling film and pierce in a couple of places. Turn your microwave to around half power and cook for 90 seconds, and leave to stand for a few more. Carefully peel back the cling film, starting with a side piece so you don't get steam burns – rare but seriously painful.

3 Add the rest of the ingredients, crumbling the stock cube into it so that it dissolves rather than sits at the bottom in a lump, and add 150ml cold water. Re-cover with cling film (remember to pierce it if you're using a new bit), and cook on full power for 3 minutes.

4 Remove, carefully uncover and stir really, really well, cover again and pop back in for another 3 minutes. Remove, carefully uncover, and leave to stand for a minute before serving. If your rice isn't cooked (just nibble a piece to check), then pop back in for 2 more minutes – not all rice is created equal. Basic white rice cooked in 6 minutes in my microwave with a 1-minute rest in the middle and a 1-minute rest at the end, but brown rice takes longer and black rice and red rice are somewhere in between. Add a tiny splash of vinegar and a pinch of salt to serve, it just makes it. Serve with yoghurt if you like.

SPRING HERB RISOTTO

SERVES 4

1 onion, finely sliced

2 fat garlic cloves, minced

2 tbsp oil

400g Arborio or long grain rice

100ml white wine

1 vegetable or chicken stock cube dissolved in 700ml boiling water

a fistful of fresh herbs (parsley, mint, dill, whatever you like), finely chopped

zest and juice of 1 lemon

When it finally feels as if spring is here, I celebrate with a great fresh herb risotto. Risotto is my favourite catch-all dinner for odds and ends in the fridge, or new-season flavours, and this one is no exception. I used parsley, mint and dill in mine, but choose the combination of herbs you prefer. It also works nicely with leftover salad leaves, such as spinach, rocket or pea shoots – there is a huge choice of greenery at this time of year.

I used chicken stock here, but a ham stock risotto with pea shoots is another favourite of mine.

1 Toss the onion and garlic into a wide, shallow pan with a little oil. Cook on low heat for about 5 minutes until it starts to soften, stirring occasionally. Add the rice and a little more oil, and crank the heat up high for a minute to toast the edges of the rice.

2 Slosh in the wine, stir, and add a generous splash of stock. Turn the heat down low again. When the stock is almost absorbed, repeat, and carry on until your rice is soupy but al dente, which may take slightly more or less stock.

3 Take the pan off the heat and fold through the herbs with the lemon zest and juice and a drizzle more oil. Rest for 5 minutes before serving.

SPUDS

I love a good tin of potatoes; when I first started writing my blog in 2012, a tin
of potatoes was 13p for 500g, or 26p a kilo, frankly far cheaper than a kilo of
fresh, loose potatoes could be found anywhere I looked. The price has risen,
five years later, but still undercuts the fresh ones by a significant margin, and
they are a handy little staple to keep kicking about in the cupboard. They pad
out a curry; stretch a pie filling; and can be knocked into a quick potato salad
or tossed with pasta, pesto and fake hard cheese for a store-cupboard pasta alla
genovese. They make perfectly passable bombay potatoes, saag aloo and sloppy
mash, too. If you absolutely can't bear the thought of buying tinned spuds, these
recipes can all be made with fresh ones, boiled and diced, instead.

CROQUETTES (V)

SERVES 4

1 x 500g tin of potatoes, drained and rinsed (350g drained weight)

a pinch of salt and a bit of cracked black pepper

100g mozzarella cheese, chopped into small chunks

a knob of butter

2 medium eggs

1 tbsp plain flour

1–2 slices of stale bread, whizzed or grated into crumbs

oil, for frying

My first introduction to the humble croquette was as a breadcrumbed mass, plucked from the deep freezer of the local supermarket and served onto my childhood dinner plates alongside baked beans and roast chicken. I would fastidiously skitter them away from the thick orange sauce lest it interfere with the satisfying crunch of the crust, the resistance and subsequent yield to my fork. Croquettes, even in their factory-made, uniform homogeny, satisfied and delighted. And then I moved away from home, and promptly forgot all about them. So keen was I to rustle up curries with my Nepalese housemate and stews for strings of lovers, that the humble croquette was forgotten. Until late 2014, when I staggered across a parmigiana variety at a restaurant in Exmouth Market, London, and my love affair was rekindled. Pulped smoky aubergines combined with buttery, creamy potatoes and bound with soft, stringy cheese.

Ordering two portions at a time became a habit; these, just these, and nothing else. They fell into fashion, and if they were on a menu, I had them, ignoring all other options. Ham and pea. Roast chicken and finely shredded cabbage. Plain potato smashed with rosemary, salt and garlic and fried in duck fat. Even a macaroni cheese version briefly graced the menu of The Butcher's Hook in Hammersmith, when I lived around the corner. Every conceivable incarnation of the rolled-up, deep-fried potato was mine, and I devoured them.

There will be those who pooh-pooh the use of tinned potatoes in this recipe; I simply ask them to give them a go. If unconvinced, replace the tinnies with pre-cooked boiled potatoes of your choosing and we'll say no more about it.

Once you know how to make a basic croquette, this gallant and gastronomic world is your small, potatoey oyster. The word croquette comes from the French word *croquer*, meaning 'to crunch', and in France they are a vehicle for leftovers, especially tomatoey, meaty ragouts and stews. Take this basic recipe and enjoy it as it stands, or make like our culinary cousins over the water and fold in your leftovers to elevate them to a delightful snack. Bliss.

1 For the best croquettes, your potatoes need to be soft and creamy-mashable. Tinned potatoes come pre-cooked, but not quite falling apart around the edges the way that they need to be, so bring a pan of water to the boil, pop in the spuds and add a pinch of salt and pepper. Reduce to a simmer for 10 minutes, or until super-soft. Remove from the heat and drain.

2 Add the mozzarella to the potatoes with the butter. Mash well to combine. Mix in one of the eggs and the flour, and pop in the fridge or stand to one side to cool.

3 Take two separate bowls, a plate and a frying pan, and prepare for the next stage while the spuds cool. In the first bowl, beat the remaining egg. Pour the breadcrumbs into the second one. Pour a little oil into the pan.

4 With floured hands, scoop up a generous tablespoon of the mixture, or two, depending on how generous you want to be. Shape it into a ball, or oblong if you prefer. Dip it into the egg bowl, then the crumbs, then set to one side on the plate. Repeat until the mixture is all used up.

5 Heat the oil over medium heat and when gently bubbling, turn the heat down to low–medium. Carefully place in each croquette and cook for 6–8 minutes, turn over, and cook for 6–8 minutes more. Remove with a slotted spoon to drain the oil and set aside. Repeat until all the croquettes are cooked.

CORNY BROWNS

SERVES 2

1 large onion, roughly diced

oil or butter, for frying

a pinch of salt and a bit of cracked black pepper

1 x 500g tin of potatoes, drained and rinsed (350g drained weight)

1 x 198g tin of sweetcorn, drained and rinsed

around 75g cheese (cheddar or hard strong cheese is best)

2 tbsp flour, plus extra for dusting

Take a tin of potatoes and a tin of sweetcorn and you can make something so much more impressive than the sum of its parts. I first made a much more hifalutin version of these as part of a consultancy job with a high-street restaurant chain, with polenta and other gubbins, but I have pared it back here to create something cheap and cheerful, quick and delicious.

A weekend breakfast staple, or dinner; make a massive pan of this and pile whatever you like on top.

1 Tip the onion into a saucepan with a little oil or butter, and season gently with salt and pepper. Cook on low heat to soften the onion and to take the acerbic edge off it, just for a few minutes, then tip into a mixing bowl.

2 Tip the spuds into the bowl. Mash them well. They might not make an actual mash, but they should crumble into chunks. This is totally fine, and will give your browns a satisfying texture, so don't worry about it too much. Add the sweetcorn and grate the cheese into the bowl. Season again, and be generous with the pepper.

3 Spoon in the flour and mix well to a thick, lumpy mixture. It should hold together and not fall off your spoon if held upside down. With floured hands, shape a little of the mixture into a patty and set to one side. Repeat until all the mixture is used up.

4 Heat a little oil in a frying pan and cook the patties for 6 minutes on each side, removing to a plate lined with a piece of kitchen roll or a clean, non-fluffy tea towel to absorb any excess oil. Repeat as required, and serve.

ALOO DUM (V)

SERVES 2

500g potatoes, diced

2 tbsp oil

1 onion, sliced

2 fat garlic cloves, finely chopped

1 red chilli, finely sliced, or a pinch of chilli flakes

½ tsp turmeric

1 tsp cumin, seeds or ground

a pinch of salt

1 large courgette, diced

1 x 400g tin of chopped tomatoes

few sprigs of fresh coriander, finely chopped

natural yoghurt, to serve (optional)

This recipe came about by a bit of experimentation. When courgettes were coming into season in the summer, I smuggled some into my aloo dum (potato curry) recipe to freshen it up, and I found it was a bit of a winner.

1 Put the potatoes in a saucepan, cover with water, bring to the boil over high heat then lower the heat and simmer for 5–6 minutes until cooked, but not tender. They should resist a fork slightly – don't overcook them as you'll carry on cooking them later. Drain.

2 Heat the oil in a large pan and add the onion, garlic and potatoes. Add the spices and salt and cook on medium heat for 10 minutes to soften the onions and crisp the edges of the potatoes.

3 Add the courgette, pour over the tomatoes and simmer for at least 15 minutes to allow the flavours to develop.

4 Garnish with finely chopped coriander. Add a dollop of natural yoghurt if you want to cool it down for kids.

TIPS

● Aloo dum more commonly uses peas than courgettes, so if you like, add a handful of frozen peas with the tomatoes instead.

● The flavours will develop the longer this dish is left, so it's great for leftovers.

TINNED SPUD FISHCAKES

MAKES 6–8,
DEPENDING ON
GENEROSITY

**1 x 500g tin of
potatoes in water,
drained and rinsed
(350g drained weight)**

**a handful of frozen
spinach, or chopped
fresh parsley**

**2 x 120g tins of
sardines in oil**

**1 tsp paprika or
tomato purée**

**2 tbsp bottled lemon
juice, or fresh if you
are so inclined**

**a pinch of salt and a
bit of cracked black
pepper**

1–2 tbsp plain flour

oil, for brushing

These fishcakes were first made for a budget food column I wrote for a couple of years until 2014, until faux-healthy bollocks and carb-shaming rolled back into fashion, and eating on a budget was swept back under the carpet. No point in reading about chia seed puddings if you can't afford the sodding ingredients, I thought, and carried on writing cheap recipes on my blog.

I was later asked to do a stint on a BBC programme on tinned food, and went for the day to a four-star hotel to play head chef to unsuspecting diners, who believed they were trying out the upmarket hotel's new menu. This was their starter, and they all enthusiastically loved it, even when the 'big reveal' at the end proved that it had been made with Sainsbury's Basics tinned potatoes and a 40p tin of sardines. At the time of filming, these fishcakes worked out at 17p per head – prices change all the time, of course, but they remain a nifty, inexpensive, filling little number. And good enough for a roomful of self-styled food connoisseurs, too.

1 The potatoes will have been pre-cooked in the tin but the best fishcakes are made with super-soft spuds, so bring a pan of water to the boil and tip them in. Reduce to a simmer and cook for around 10 minutes, until they fall apart easily. If using frozen spinach, pop it in a sieve and balance it on top of the pan as the potatoes cook, to defrost it. Prod it with a fork to break it up and help it along.

2 Drain the spuds and tip them back into the pan.

3 Open the tins of sardines and carefully pour the oil in and mash the potatoes to a pulp with either a fork or a masher. Give it a brisk beating – a wooden spoon can help matters along if they won't play ball.

Recipe continues overleaf

4 When you have achieved a rough mash, tip in the sardines. Flake them with the side of a fork, bones and all, as the bones are full of calcium and goodness. If you are concerned about them – and some people are – then just remove any visible ones to put your mind at rest. They generally tend to be soft and mashable and not pose a danger, but you do what is best for you.

5 Mix the lot together, with the paprika and defrosted spinach or fresh parsley, the lemon juice, a pinch of salt and a generous amount of pepper. If you don't tend to have paprika lying around (it's more for colour than flavour, to temper what looks like a greying mass), add a squeeze of tomato purée instead.

6 Beat in 1 tablespoon of flour until the mixture is stiff, not sloppy. Test it by scooping some on your spoon and holding it upside down. If it stays in place, you're good to go. If it slops off, you need a little more flour.

7 Pop the mixture in the fridge for at least half an hour to firm; this stops the fishcakes falling apart in the pan. If you're in a huge hurry you can add an egg and another tablespoon of flour at this stage and skip the fridge, but it really does make a difference. I get it though, sometimes you just want dinner and you want it now, or there's hungry toddlers tugging on legs, or similar.

8 When they are good to go, preheat the oven to 180°C/350°F/gas 4. Lightly grease a baking sheet and, with floured hands, take 2 generous tablespoons of the mixture. Roll it into a ball and flatten gently, then pop on the baking sheet. Repeat until all of the mixture is used up, making 6–8 fishcakes.

9 Brush them with a little oil to help them crisp, and pop in the oven for around 15 minutes, or until golden. And ta-dah, gourmet dinner, from a tin.

TIP

● You can also make these into small meatball-sized balls instead, which I do sometimes; my Small Boy hooted with laughter the first time I told him we were having Fishy Balls for tea!

MOONSHINE MASH (V)

SERVES 4,
OR DOESN'T . . .

**500g potatoes,
finely sliced**

**a pinch of salt and a
bit of cracked black
pepper**

**½ x 300g tin of
sweetcorn, drained
(around 100g drained
weight)**

**a generous knob of
butter**

**a grating of nutmeg
(optional)**

**a good grating of
strong cheese,
to taste**

This recipe came around completely by accident, as so many of
the best of them do. I was recovering from a throat infection and
hankering for something soft and soothing, so I started to make
myself a pile of mashed potatoes. And then one of my readers sent
me a recipe from the *New York Times* for a buttery polenta topped with
mushrooms. It was not dissimilar to a dish I had eaten in Palomar,
Soho, and greatly enjoyed, but my spuds were already boiling and I
didn't have any polenta to hand. I'm not sure I ever have done. I tried to
make do with mashed potatoes, but the seed of sweet creamy corn
had been planted, and so I turfed half a tin of sweetcorn into my mash
and pulverised it. And, oh, I'm so glad I did. This recipe should ideally
serve four as a side dish or a base to a main, but, well, mine didn't . . .

Recipe continues overleaf

1 Toss the potatoes into a saucepan, cover them with cold water, chuck in a good pinch of salt and bring to the boil. Reduce to a simmer on medium–low heat and cook for around 10 minutes, until the potatoes are very soft. You can test them by poking a sharp knife or fork into the pan – if they yield with no resistance, they're good to go.

2 When the potatoes are cooked, drain the corn and toss it into the pan. Heat for another minute or two – the warmer corn will be easier to work with.

3 Drain the lot and tip back into the pan. Add the butter, a generous pinch of pepper and the nutmeg, if using. Mash vigorously until roughly smooth, using a fork or potato masher.

4 Stir in the grated cheese to evenly combine. Serve piping hot, and generously.

TIP

● To make this vegan, simply replace the cheese with a strong vegan alternative, or leave it out altogether and add a little more salt.

BEANS, PULSES, LENTILS

The *Guardian* once wrote a profile piece naming me as 'the face of modern poverty', an accolade I neither asked for nor quite fit, as modern poverty has many faces: the elderly and forgotten, the newborn, of every colour, almost every postcode, not just mine. But in the article I expressed exasperation at the often well-meant advice from onlookers, 'you just need a bag of lentils'. Lentils and dried pulses were an unknown thing to me, and when you've scrabbled £1 from armchairs and pavements outside nightclubs, the last thing you want is to blow it on tasteless slop that might end up in the bin. So I shrank from them until I had a little more money and culinary confidence to explore.

Fast forward four years and I have jars of pulses jostling for space on my shelf. I've researched and experimented, so you can pick up a bag of beans or lentils safe in the knowledge that these recipes have been rigorously tested. A bag of lentils certainly won't solve poverty, but it helps to have one kicking around in lean times to pull together a quick, healthy dinner.

BEST EVER NUT BURGER (VE)

MAKES 6 GENEROUS
FAT BURGERS

**200g mixed shelled
nuts**

oil, for frying

a pinch of salt

**1 large onion, finely
chopped**

**4 fat garlic cloves,
finely chopped
(optional)**

**200g mushrooms,
thinly sliced**

**a few pinches of
mixed dried herbs**

**1 x 400g tin of kidney
beans or chickpeas,
drained and rinsed**

1 tbsp lemon juice

**a pinch of chilli flakes
(optional)**

**2 tbsp plain flour,
plus extra for dusting**

One of my first forays into a professional kitchen was the inimitable Blackfoot, in Exmouth Market, in London, and one of my favourite recipes was their nut burger – a pleasant surprise to any vegetarian guests at the pork palace! The original recipe was itself based on a nut roast from Allegra McEvedy's *Big Table Busy Kitchen*, incarnated into a burger, fiddled with by me, and this is the version I make for myself at home, which bears just enough resemblance to the original to be considered a tribute.

I put mushrooms in mine in place of the original chestnuts, and onions for the leeks, because mushrooms and onions are generally in my fridge, and chestnuts and leeks rarely so. This is also a great place for leftover Christmas nuts, if you have them lying around; just crack the lot and make something of them instead of letting them gather dust in a bowl on the side. You know who you are!

1 Tip the nuts into a large pan with a splash of oil and a pinch of salt over medium heat for a few minutes, stirring to gently toast them. When the edges start to go a bit golden, quickly remove them and tip them into your blender. Pulse for half a minute, shake to loosen, and repeat until they are ground down. Some larger pieces remaining are fine – I like a bit of texture. Tip them into a bowl and set to one side.

2 Now back to your pan. Toss the onion, garlic and mushrooms into the pan with the herbs on low heat and a splash more oil if needed. Cook for a few minutes to soften. Add the beans to the pan, along with the nuts, lemon juice and chilli flakes, if you like. Remove from the heat and mash everything together thoroughly to form a thick paste. Add the flour and mix well to thicken and bind it.

3 Transfer the mix into a bowl, cover and chill in the fridge for at least 30 minutes. This stage is super-important; if you skip it your burger mix will fall to a smoosh in the pan. Let it all cool, thicken and bind itself together and ignore it. Wash up. Call a friend you haven't spoken to in a while. Just leave that burger mix alone.

4 When The Time Has Come, remove it from the fridge and shape it into balls with floured hands. Pop a little oil in your pan, heat it up high (but not smoking, you've come this far, this is not the time to set fire to your kitchen) and place a few in, flattening with a fork to form your burger shape. Cook for 6 minutes on one side, until they come away from the pan cleanly without falling apart, and the same on the other, turning the heat down a little to keep it under control. And serve. I've served these up as part of a vegan Sunday roast before now, to six people, with only one vegan present – and everyone loved it.

TIP

● These are also great in a bun with some sort of chutney, or the mix makes great nut-balls, too. Leftover patties can be stored in the fridge for 3 days or frozen for 3 months.

BEET HUMMUS AND FLATBREAD (VE)

MAKES 8, SERVES
AROUND 4

**FOR THE
FLATBREADS**

**250g plain flour, plus
extra for dusting**

250g wholemeal flour

**1 tsp fast-action
dried yeast**

**1 tbsp granulated
sugar**

1 tsp salt

300ml warm water

FOR THE HUMMUS

**300g beetroot, peeled
and quartered**

**4 tbsp oil (I used
groundnut), plus
extra for roasting
the beetroot**

**300g tinned
chickpeas, drained
and rinsed**

**2 fat garlic cloves,
roughly chopped**

1 tbsp pumpkin seeds

This colourful hummus is a cheering addition to sandwiches, party tables and lunchboxes. I like to poke at mine with cucumber sticks or homemade flatbread. The chickpeas can be replaced with any white pulse, such as haricot beans, if you like.

1 **Preheat the oven to 180°C/350°F/gas 4.**

2 **Mix together the flours, yeast, sugar and salt in a large bowl. Make a well (a sort of hole) in the centre and add 250ml of the water. Combine to a soft dough, adding more water if necessary. Knead the dough well on a floured work surface – you'll feel it smooth and soften as you go. Divide it into eight balls and place on a baking tray, cover with a tea towel and leave to rise for 1 hour.**

3 **Meanwhile, put the beetroot in a roasting tin with a splash of oil. Cook in the centre of the oven for about 30 minutes, until soft and slightly crisp around the edges, then remove and allow to cool.**

4 **Turn up the oven to 220°C/425°F/gas 7.**

5 **Put the chickpeas into a blender with the garlic and oil. Pulse, add the beetroot and pulse again, adding a splash of water if necessary. Spoon into ramekins, top with pumpkin seeds, cover and chill in the fridge.**

6 **When the flatbread dough has doubled in size, knock back each ball and roll out on a lightly floured surface to around 3mm deep. Place on a floured baking tray and cook for 6 minutes in the oven, until slightly puffed and golden around the edges. Cut into strips and serve with the hummus.**

BLACK BEAN TARKARI (VE)

1 large onion, finely sliced

4 fat garlic cloves, crushed

a pinch of salt

2 tbsp oil

1 tsp cumin seeds

1 tsp ground coriander (dhaniya powder)

½ tsp turmeric

2 pinches of chilli flakes

1 x 247g tin of peaches in fruit juice or syrup

2 tbsp tomato purée

1 x 400g tin of black beans

a drop of lemon juice

fresh coriander or parsley, to serve (optional)

This recipe was, in part, inspired by a tarkari dish on the menu of my local Nepalese takeaway, Yak and Yeti. I had moved back to Southend from the dizzy heights of the busy big City, finished lugging several car-boots of boxes up two flights of stairs, and before I knew it, it was late and I was hungry. Rather than locate the box with the kitchen equipment in, I picked up a pile of the take-away menus that litter the hallways of a vacant home, and rifled through. Yak and Yeti caught my eye, if only for the name, and a curiosity about Nepalese cuisine. I made it myself some months later, substituting their chicken with my own tin of black beans, and it was a triumph.

The original recipe uses mango, but mine uses tinned peaches, as they are cheaper. For the real deal, sling a sliced mango in, too, but I've had both and they are equally splendid.

Recipe continues overleaf

1 Toss the onion and garlic into a pan with a pinch of salt and the oil over low heat to gently soften the onions. Don't be tempted to turn the heat up too high for speed, as you will burn the garlic, it is a delicate soul.

2 After a few minutes, add the cumin seeds, dhaniya powder, turmeric and chilli flakes and stir well to coat the onions.

3 Drain the peaches and reserve the juice or syrup to add in later to taste; for some, the peaches alone will be quite sweet enough, but I admit to enjoying the saccharine sweetness of the juice thrown in, too, to temper the heat of the spices. Add a splash of water, and the tomato purée, and bring to the boil.

4 Boil vigorously for a minute, then reduce to a simmer for 20 minutes, or until the peaches have softened. If the liquid starts to dry out, add in the reserved peach juice or a splash of water, and stir well. Break up the peaches with a fork or masher, and stir.

5 When the sauce is ready (thick, roughly textured), drain and rinse the black beans. Fold through with the lemon juice and cook for a further 5 minutes to warm through. Serve with fresh coriander or parsley as a garnish, or not, if you don't keep that kind of thing hanging around.

BLACK BEAN SAUCE (VE)

MAKES A SIZEABLE
JAR

**1 x 400g tin of black
beans, drained and
rinsed**

a few pinches of salt

1 tbsp any vinegar

**4 fat garlic cloves,
sliced**

2 tbsp oil

**200ml vegetable
stock (homemade or
use a stock cube)**

**2 tbsp soy sauce
(optional)**

2 tsp sugar

2 tsp any flour

a pinch of chilli flakes

As ever, I'm taking a marginal amount of liberty with this recipe, to simplify it while trying to keep it pretty close to the real deal. Authentic black bean sauce calls for 'fermented black soy beans', whereas I've found I can get pretty damn close with a pinch of salt and a dash of lemon juice, left overnight to do its thing. Fermenting beans is fun, but a long process; I once fermented red beans to make gochujang paste – a hot Korean sauce – and although I don't regret it, I'm not in the habit of waiting six months for my dinner. If you're curious, there are many good tutorials online – take a look and see if it's for you. In the meantime, here's my simple version, with no half-year waiting period.

1 Tip the beans into a non-metallic bowl or container. Cover with cold water, the salt (don't be alarmed, you'll rinse them again) and a dash of vinegar, cover the bowl and pop it in the fridge overnight.

2 Rinse the beans thoroughly and set to one side. Toss the garlic into a pan with the oil and the rinsed beans over low heat, so as not to burn the garlic, and cook for a few minutes to soften.

3 Add the veg stock, the soy sauce, if using, and sugar and bring to the boil, then reduce to a simmer for a few minutes until the beans start to split and break down.

4 Tip the lot into a blender, add the flour and chilli and pulse to a liquid. You may need to add a little more water – not all beans are created equal – but you do want quite a thick sauce. Pour back into the pan and cook on low–medium heat for 10 minutes to thicken.

5 If you are using this immediately, set it to one side and stir-fry some veg of your choice, then pour over the sauce a few minutes before serving. If you are saving it for future use, allow to cool completely and decant into clean containers, then pop them in the freezer until required.

AUBERGINE AND LENTIL VINDALOO (VE)

SERVES 2-4,
DEPENDING ON
APPETITE

**1 large aubergine or
2 small ones, diced**

salt

50g dried red lentils

3 onions, finely sliced

oil, for frying

4 fat garlic cloves

**½ tsp ground
cinnamon**

**1 tsp cumin, seeds
or ground**

**¼ star anise, or
⅛ tsp fennel seeds**

**a good grind of black
pepper, and then
another one**

1–2 tsp chilli flakes

2 tbsp tomato purée

**2 tbsp vinegar or
lemon juice, fresh
or bottled**

a fistful of spinach

I knocked up this hottie in my little kitchen after a few weeks of new-veganism. (I should rewrite that, but I'm not going to.) I had been working my way through a list of curries, partly for this book, partly for a challenge, as I had a jokey conversation with a few friends on Instagram about doing 'a year of curry', and partly because there are so many things I enjoy but have never tried to cook myself. And so, vindaloo.

I delved into one of my curry bibles, Camellia Panjabi's *50 Great Curries of India*, and, of course, there on page 102 was a vindaloo recipe. Admittedly with lamb, but I substitute lamb with aubergine in recipes as a rule, and I rolled up my sleeves and started to make notes. The original recipe called for cinnamon, an innocuous store-cupboard staple that I had donated to my Nan a few days before for her roast potatoes, no less. (And I always wondered what made them so special!) And cloves, that I bought for Christmas and couldn't find anywhere, the blighters. I last remember crunching on a few in the bathroom to deal with a toothache, but they weren't in there either. Mind you, I no longer have the nefarious toothache, so perhaps in my delirious agony I munched the lot. Anyway, I replaced the cloves with star anise and cumin, and it was delicious.

If you don't like aubergine, use mushrooms instead. Red lentils could easily be kidney beans, baked beans, black beans, brown or green lentils, or yellow split peas; whatever you have in the cupboard or like. They are here to add texture and protein; all the other flavour speaks for itself, or rather, shouts and sings and dances.

Recipe continues overleaf

1 Sprinkle the chopped aubergine with a generous pinch of salt in a bowl, then set aside.

2 Thoroughly rinse the lentils and place them in a pan. Cover them with water – no salt or the lentils will take an age to cook – and bring to the boil. I was initially tempted to throw them into the pot to make this a one-pot dinner, but lentils produce so much 'scum' that rises to the top of the pan, I didn't want to mar my beautiful adventure, so doubled my washing up ... When the water is boiling, reduce to a simmer for around 12 minutes until soft and swollen. Drain, rinse well to knock off the scum, and set aside.

3 Meanwhile, toss the onions into a large pan with a little oil and over medium heat soften the onions for 10 minutes. Add the garlic cloves, peeled, but whole, and the salted aubergine, stirring to stop it from sticking and burning. Cook for 15 minutes, adding more oil if needed.

4 Add the cinnamon, cumin, star anise or fennel, and pepper, but only half of your chosen quantity of chilli. It is easy to add to, but rather more difficult to temper down if you misjudge it, so I put half the chilli in to cook, and leave half to garnish. It means guests and dining partners can choose their own heat, too, which is ideal if everyone is a little different. Stir well to combine, then add 200ml water to the pan, and crank up the heat to medium–high. It doesn't look brilliant right now but trust me, it gets better.

5 Add the reserved lentils, tomato purée and vinegar or lemon juice and stir well. Bring to the boil, then reduce to a simmer and cover, stirring slowly and therapeutically every now and then. It should take around 30 minutes to meld into this glossy, orange, spicy goodness, and the liquid should thicken to an unctuous sauce. If it is too watery, bring it back to the boil, then reduce the heat and cook a little more. Stir through the spinach a few minutes before serving. And ta-dah, you're done! It would also be delicious with simple boiled rice to make it go a little further.

I CANNOT GET ENOUGH OF THIS FIVE-MINUTE THING (VE)

SERVES 2

FOR THE DRESSING

2 tbsp peanut butter (or other nut or seed butter)

60ml oil

a pinch of salt and a bit of cracked black pepper

scant ¼ tsp any kind of mustard

1 tbsp bottled lemon juice or zest and juice of ½ small one

a pinch of chilli flakes or cayenne pepper

AND THE REST

100g frozen spinach

6 fat garlic cloves

½ onion of any colour (we are not onion-fascists round here), finely diced

1–2 large tomatoes, or a generous fistful of babies (not actual babies. Please don't eat babies), roughly chopped

1 x 400g tin of chickpeas or other legume, drained and rinsed

One afternoon in the all-hours flail-and-flurry that was writing this glorious book, I emerged from my writing corner (apologies to Virginia Woolf for not managing an entire 'room of my own in which to write' but, recession, gentrification and a dislike of cleaning mean I basically live in a nook. Anyway, when there is a small child around, all rooms are rightfully theirs and filled with plastic horror and there is no fighting it). I digress. I emerged from my corner (hungry) and hulked to my fridge (empty). Rummaged in the cupboard. So many of my favourite recipes begin this way. To cut a slightly rubbish story short, five minutes later I was photographing this for my blog before swiftly devouring it. Enjoy. And always keep a tin of chickpeas in your cupboard and a bag of something green and leafy in your freezer.

This is even better the next day when it has been lolling around in the fridge, so make double and eat it for a couple of days – it's a great quick lunch and as the title suggests, I seriously cannot get enough of it.

1 Grab a jar with a good lid. Put the dressing ingredients in it and screw on said lid. Shake it all about like you're Tom Cruise, either in *Cocktail* or leaping up and down on the Oprah sofa, your shout. Remove lid. Dip a finger in. Yummy, isn't it? If you disagree, add some more of something to balance it to your liking. Set to one side.

2 Pop the frozen spinach in a small bowl. Top and tail the garlic (chop the gnarly end off the bottom of the clove and the pointy bit off the top) and stab all the way through with the tip of your knife. Put in another small bowl. Pop both in the microwave for 3 x 20-second bursts. Your garlic should resemble roasted garlic, one of my favourite lazy cooking tricks, and the spinach should be mostly defrosted. Fling the spinach back in the microwave for a minute. Pop the garlic out of its skins and set aside.

3 Fling the onion and tomatoes into a bowl. Add the chickpeas, stir in the spinach and garlic. Throw the dressing over the lot. Give it a good mix, season to taste, and enjoy. I like mine coolish, but it's lovely hot as well.

BEANS AND GREENS GUARDIAN SALAD (VE)

SERVES 4 FOR LUNCH

1 fat garlic clove

a pinch of chilli flakes

100ml oil

2 tbsp lemon juice

100g dried brown, green or red lentils

1 x 400g tin of black-eyed or haricot beans

2 large tomatoes, finely diced

100g kale or other green leaf, chopped and tough stalks removed

a handful of black olives

a fistful of fresh parsley, chopped (optional)

Move over kale pesto, there's a new kid in town. When I first made this recipe for my *Guardian* column, it was dubbed 'the most *Guardian* recipe ever'; although the tongue-in-cheek title didn't make it past the sub-editors, it's always remained that in my head. It is worth making plenty, as the leftovers are perfect for taking to work to scoff at your desk. It is best served at room temperature, so it doesn't matter if you forget to take it out of your bag or fridge space is at a premium (or you have the kind of colleagues that pilfer good-looking lunches).

If you can, warm the dressing before tossing it through the salad to soften the kale and ensure it clings to the beans. Then eat hot, cold or somewhere in between. Look out for olives sold in a tin, rather than in the tiny delicatessen snack-packs – they may be a little broken but they're often much cheaper and are perfect for something like this.

1 First make the dressing – put the garlic clove and chilli into a lidded jar and pour over the oil and some of the lemon juice. A good steeping in oil and acid will calm the chilli and garlic and meld the flavours.

2 Screw on the lid tightly and shake vigorously to emulsify. Unscrew, taste and adjust with more lemon juice, if needed. The dressing is best when made a day in advance, but perfectly acceptable fresh if you're not that organised.

3 When you're ready to make the salad, thoroughly rinse the lentils and put them in a pan of unsalted cold water. Bring to the boil, scrape off any scum and boil vigorously for 10 minutes. Reduce to a simmer and cook for a further 10 minutes, or until tender. Red lentils will cook quickly, whereas green and brown ones take a little longer.

4 Drain and rinse the beans and toss in to warm through, then drain the lot. Toss the other salad ingredients together with the pulses. Add the dressing to taste and serve.

TINDADE

MAKES A LOT

300ml whole milk

a few generous pinches of salt and a grinding of black pepper (optional)

a pinch or two of mixed dried herbs

4 x 125g tins of mackerel

1 x 330g tin of new potatoes in water

1 x 400g tin of white beans (cannellini or haricots are best)

up to 50ml oil

1 tbsp lemon juice

I had my first brandade a couple of years ago at St John Bread and Wine in London – there was a party of some sort going on, and I spent most of the evening skulking shyly in corners and corridors, terrified of a roomful of my culinary heroes and worried I would make a twit out of myself. Luckily the corner I chose to lurk in was the one that the kitchen used to ferry platters to the party, so my social recalcitrance paid off in salt cod brandade and other assorted morsels.

This brandade is nothing like that one, I'm afraid, as I have neither the skill nor the flair of the great Fergus Henderson, but it's a good memory, and I need to write them down somewhere. My cookbooks are essentially my drip-fed memoirs played out in small plates and large knives. So, with apologies to the whole of France for my cultural in-appropriation, here's how to make my extremely bastardised version of a classic. After all, as a woman once told me, 'you don't cook, you just take stuff out of tins and sling it together'. Quite. This is my version with tinned mackerel and spuds. Hence Tindade. Fergus, I'm sorry I even mentioned you on the same page as this abomination. I really am.

1 Grab a wide, shallow pan, if you have one, if not, any medium pan will do, and set over low heat, then add the milk, salt and a pinch of herbs.

2 Prise open the tins of fish, remove the lids completely, and remove those usefully large ring pulls (see Tip!). Pop the fish in the milk pan – tinned fish is usually boneless, but if you spot any, just remove them carefully.

3 Open the tin of potatoes (see Tip), drain and rinse well. Quarter the potatoes and toss them into the pan with the fish, then give everything a stir. Drain and rinse the beans and add those too. The tinned goods will already have been cooked, but they will be easier to work into a soft mash if everything is a little warm. Bring the heat up to medium, and keep an eye for 5 minutes, stirring to disturb so the ingredients don't stick and burn.

4 Place a sieve or colander over a mixing bowl or another pan and tip the contents into it, catching the liquid below. Transfer it back into the original pan and mash well, adding the milk and oil a little at a time to soften. Opinions are divided on this – I like my brandade smooth and spreadable, some people like theirs rough and chunky – so there's no right or wrong end product.

5 When you're happy with it, add the lemon juice, mix well, taste it – add more salt, some pepper, more herbs or lemon as you see fit, and enjoy. I like mine eaten with a spoon in a moment of laziness, but a hefty dollop next to a soft-boiled or poached egg for breakfast is pretty special, too. This will keep in the fridge, stored in a jar with a scant layer of oil on top, for up to 4 days, and in the freezer for a month.

TIPS

● The ring pulls from fish tins come in handy for hanging clothes hangers one beneath the other to dry clothes, pair outfits or save on storage space. I digress, but this is a genuinely useful thing, and ring pulls are everywhere, so keep 'em.

● The large potato tins are handy, too – I use mine to split and re-pot herbs, as desk tidies and general receptacles for junk around the house. Two upturned are a fab pair of bongos for a small child – he paints them as a rainy-day activity – or stab a couple of holes in, thread with long string and walk around the house on your new funny feet.

DEEP-FRIED SPICY CHICKPEAS (VE)

1 x 400g tin of chickpeas

100ml oil

FOR THE SPICE MIX

1 tbsp salt

2 tbsp smoked paprika

grated zest of 1 whole lemon

1 tbsp brown sugar

1 tbsp dried mixed herbs or thyme

These are an excellent snack for afternoon movies, buffet lunches (read: knocked-together toot from the fridge), and to top curries and stews with; I first made them as part of a taste test for a well-known high street restaurant chain. They didn't make them onto their menu, which is good news really, as it means I can share them with you all here. I make these regularly at home, varying the spices, and the trick is to cook them until they are really properly crisp.

1 Rinse and drain the chickpeas and tip onto a plate/into a bowl lined with kitchen roll or a clean non-fluffy tea towel to gently dry.

2 Heat a few centimetres of oil in a small deep pan (keep it small to use less oil), until gently bubbling – tip in the chickpeas and turn down the heat.

3 Combine the spice mix ingredients and put them in a bowl. When the peas start to float, lift them out with a slotted spoon, drop them into the spices and shake to coat. Best eaten hot, but still nice cold.

TARKA DAAL (VE)

SERVES 4 AS A SIDE
OR 2 AS A MAIN

**250g dried red lentils
or yellow split peas
– or any other small
pulse of your choice**

1 tsp turmeric

**a pinch of salt and a
bit of cracked black
pepper**

2 onions, finely sliced

**6 fat garlic cloves,
finely chopped**

**a small piece of fresh
root ginger, finely
chopped**

2 tbsp oil, for frying

**2 tsp cumin, seeds or
ground**

**½ tsp English
mustard**

**1 tbsp tomato purée,
or 1 fresh large
tomato, finely diced**

**a fistful of fresh
coriander, chopped,
to serve**

**a few pinches of chilli
flakes, to taste**

I am yet to meet a tarka daal that I have not fallen in love with, and this says less about my fickle and romantic nature and more about the soft, sweet, unctuous consistency of one of my most favourite comfort foods. Locally I must pay tribute to the excellent Keralam, and the Mamataz Mahal Tandoori, both staples for my daal fix for long nights and eaten cold the next morning. When I am working in the City I often seek out my nearest stall of spicy goodness – too many to recall let alone name – finding a homely comfort in the familiar sloppy softness of sweet garlic and onions, mustard seeds and cumin and an assortment of pulses. All the better served in a styrofoam cup and wrapped in a few sheets of a newspaper found on the Underground to keep it – and me – warm. In the rare cases where I don't gobble the lot up greedily, I fold leftovers into gramcake batter (see page 68) and into pies and pasties.

COOKING ON A BOOTSTRAP

1 First soak the pulses; this may seem unnecessary but it saves on the cooking time. The best daals are achieved when the pulses break right down into a soft, creamy soupiness, which can be achieved after either a couple of hours of cooking, or an overnight soak and a faster cook.

2 Rinse the pulses under the cold tap, drain and pop into a pan. Add 1.2 litres of water and bring to the boil, skimming off any scum that rises to the surface. Reduce to a simmer and toss in the turmeric and a pinch of pepper.

3 Meanwhile, add the onions, garlic and ginger to a frying pan with the oil, cumin and mustard. Cook slowly and gently for a few minutes to soften and tip into the pan of lentils.

4 Cook for 45 minutes to 1 hour, until the pulses have broken down and the daal has thickened. I like mine thick and soupy, you may wish to add a splash of water to loosen it, if you like. Stir through the tomato purée or diced tomato. Season to taste with salt and pepper, garnish with chopped fresh coriander and chilli flakes, and serve.

MAKHANI DAAL (VE)

SERVES 4 AS A SIDE
DISH OR 2 AS A MAIN

**100g dried brown or
black lentils**

**1 large red or white
onion, finely chopped**

**4 fat garlic cloves,
finely chopped**

**a few thin slices of
fresh ginger root,
finely chopped**

**1 small red chilli,
finely sliced, or a
pinch of chilli flakes**

**2 tbsp oil, for frying
(not olive oil!)**

1 tsp turmeric

2 tsp ground cumin

a pinch of salt

**1 x 400g tin of kidney
beans in water,
drained and rinsed
(approx 250g drained
weight)**

2 tbsp tomato purée

**a fistful of fresh
coriander (or spinach
or parsley)**

Last year, I visited Bolton, Lancashire, on the way to the Lake District, stopping for dinner and a snooze to break up the very long journey from home to Cumbria. I left the guest house in search of an infamous Lancashire hotpot, but there were none to be found anywhere that we looked. Instead, we found Spice Valley, an Indian restaurant with such delights as Rabbit Varuval, Curried Scallops and Makhani Daal on their menu – and feasted on new and exciting ideas. The one I loved most was Makhani Daal, a simple side dish of kidney beans and black lentils, and I set about making my own when I got back home.

1 Rinse the lentils and pop them in a small pan of cold water – with no salt yet, or they'll take an age to cook. Bring the water to the boil, then reduce to a simmer for 15–20 minutes. Brown and black lentils hold their shape when cooked, unlike red ones, which turn translucent and eventually fall apart.

2 Toss the onion, garlic, ginger and chilli into a large pan with the oil, add the turmeric and cumin and a pinch of salt, and cook on low heat for 10 minutes to soften.

3 Add the beans to the onions with 400ml water and the tomato purée. Stir, and crank the heat up to bring it to the boil. When boiling, reduce the heat to a simmer and cook for 15 minutes, stirring occasionally.

4 When the kidney beans start to soften and break down, mash them with a fork or masher and stir well, repeating until they are more of a purée than a bean. Not all kidney beans are created equal, I find the cheaper tins contain broken and split beans so they break down more easily, whereas the premium brands are hardier things and take longer to cook. You can speed up the process by tipping it all into a blender or food processor, if you have one, but this is one of those dishes I like to stand and idly stir, rather like risotto, I find it soothing to stand still for a while in my busy days.

5 When the daal is thickened, whether by daydreaming or by blender, drain the lentils and fold them through the bean mix. Roughly chop some coriander (or spinach or parsley if you dislike coriander) and scatter on top to serve.

ONION AND LENTIL KORMA (VE)

MAKES 2 GENEROUS PORTIONS

2 onions, finely sliced

4 garlic cloves, chopped

2 tbsp oil

150g dried red lentils

½ tsp turmeric

1 tsp cumin, seeds or ground

a scant pinch of chilli flakes

200g coconut cream

100g frozen spinach

a fistful of sultanas

2 tsp tomato purée (optional)

1 tbsp lemon juice

a pinch of salt and a bit of cracked black pepper

Regular readers will know I love a curry, especially as a warm and satisfying meal to encompass whatever happens to be kicking around in the fridge or cupboard on a particularly lean day. This one has become something of a staple for the last few onions in the fridge and the rest of a bag of lentils, so it helps to always have a bag of frozen greens and a carton of coconut cream on standby. Coconut cream is coconut milk's underrated little sibling; it's thicker, so it goes further, and it's usually cheaper, too. Since I discovered it, I haven't bought coconut milk at all.

1 Toss the onion and garlic into a wide pan with the oil. Over low heat, slowly soften the onions and garlic; you don't want to burn them at this stage, or the burnt taste will permeate your whole dish, so take it slow and stir frequently to stop them sticking.

2 Thoroughly rinse the lentils and, when the onion has started to soften, add them to the pan, with the spices and 250ml water. Bring to the boil, skimming off any scum that rises to the surface and discarding it, and reduce the heat. Add the coconut cream and simmer for 20 minutes, stirring well.

3 When the lentils have absorbed most of the liquid, add 250ml water, along with the frozen spinach, sultanas and tomato purée, if using, and stir. Heat and add more water until the lentils are cooked to your liking; some people like them with a little crunch, others soft, swollen and translucent.

4 When ready to serve, dress with a little lemon juice to lift it; the coconut cream can be quite sweet and heavy, and a dash of lemon juice makes all the difference. Season to taste with salt and pepper if you use them, and serve.

BEETBURGERS (VE)

2 beetroots, grated

**1 large onion of any
colour, finely chopped**

2 tbsp oil

**1 tsp cumin, seeds
or ground**

½ tsp turmeric

½ tsp paprika

a pinch of salt

a dash of vinegar

**2 x 400g tins of
kidney beans,
drained and rinsed**

3 tbsp plain flour

I love the general enthusiasm that Veganuary generates across my social media (an annual challenge to try vegan for January), and in 2017 with 40,000 people signing up and support from Stella McCartney and other fabulous animal lovers, the buzz created was gorgeously warm and supportive.

These beetburgers have been created with Veganuary in mind. Not to be confused with my Beetballs, these pack a serious protein punch and are simple to make. I always wear rubber gloves to handle beetroots, to prevent Lady Macbeth hands, but also as I run my hands through my hair in exasperation five hundred times a day, it stops me accidentally dyeing chunks of it pink in the process …

1 Pop the grated beetroot in a big wide frying pan. Toss in the onion, too. Add 1 tablespoon of the oil and cook on gentle heat for around 10 minutes to soften, stirring constantly to disturb it all so it doesn't stick and burn.

2 Add the spices, season with salt and a dash of vinegar (any vinegar will do, I use boring old malt but fancypants stuff will just make it even better if you keep it kicking about) and stir well to combine. Remove from the heat for a moment.

3 Tip the kidney beans into the pan and return to the heat. Mash well, keeping everything moving, until it comes together in a rough paste. Remove from the heat and stir in the flour until relatively stiff. If you pick up a dollop on your spoon and hold it upside down, it should hold fast.

4 Grab a baking tray and very lightly grease it. Pick up a heaped spoon of the mixture and pat it into a patty with floured hands. Place it on the baking tray, and repeat until all of the mixture is used up. Err on the side of thinner burgers, as they cook faster, and you can always layer them up for a bigger bite! Pop the tray in the freezer for 10 minutes or the fridge for half an hour, uncovered, to firm up the burgers. This step is important, as otherwise you could end up with a pan of hot moosh. I mean, it'll be super-tasty hot moosh, it just won't be a burger, so it depends on where your priorities are!

5 I use these 10 minutes to clear down the surfaces and quickly wash up ... ha ha ha ha who am I kidding, I fanny around on Twitter and act surprised when the washing up doesn't do itself! Wipe your pan down at least, though, because you'll need it again in a moment, but it has the same stuff going back into it so it doesn't need to be spotless.

6 When the patties have lounged around a while and are nice and firm to (gently) touch, heat the remaining oil in the pan. Add a few burgers at a time, being careful not to overcrowd the pan as it makes them tricky to turn over, and cook for 5 minutes on medium heat on each side.

7 Remove from the pan and repeat as required. They freeze well, cooked or uncooked, or can be kept in the fridge for up to 3 days. I had one tonight in a burger bun and have destined another to be broken into chunks with salad and (vegan) mayo in a flatbread tomorrow. Enjoy! And remember to tag me in them if you make them – I love seeing all of your cooking!

TIP

● The turmeric is not essential; if you don't have it in, don't buy it especially – I just sling it in everything as it is supposed to be excellent for inflammation and my sodding arthritis needs all the help it can get – please note, I am not recommending this as medical advice and my Doctorate is merely honorary!

BEETBALLS! (VE)

MAKES 20

200g dried red lentils

1 small onion, finely sliced

2 fat garlic cloves, finely sliced

150g cooked beetroot (not the kind in vinegar), finely diced

2 tbsp oil, plus extra for drizzling

½ tsp cumin or coriander, seeds or ground

1 slice of bread or a pitta

a pinch of salt

1 tbsp lemon juice, fresh or bottled

These beetballs are based on a beetroot burger recipe from Lee Watson's incredible vegan recipe book, *Peace and Parsnips*. If you follow my social media, you might have seen me evangelise about this book once or twice; in fact, such is my vim and vigour for this beautiful culinary bible that I once put it on the desk of the country's best food magazine with an insistence that it was read first out of the hundreds of books piled up there. I have given copies to friends, new and old vegans alike, carnivores, and today thrust my own copy at my friend Jane with corners folded down and jabbing a finger at the photos, asking her how she could refuse a beetroot burger from a man who looks like Jesus himself. So thank you, Lee, for the inspiration for these beetballs – I started off making your burgers and got carried away. Apologies that they aren't in their original incarnation, but here we are.

For a gluten-free version, simply replace the slice of bread with a tablespoon or two of your preferred gluten-free flour; it's just to bind the ingredients together to hold them in shape. Add one and see how firm it is, then add a little more if required.

1 Thoroughly rinse your lentils under a cold tap, then pop into a pan. Cover with water and bring to the boil; do not add any salt at this stage or your lentils may seize and never ever soften. Sad but true. Reduce to a simmer and cook for around 15 minutes, until very soft, swollen and translucent.

2 Meanwhile, toss the onion and garlic into a pan. Finely dice your beetroot and add that, too. Add the oil and spice of your choice, and soften over medium heat, stirring regularly to stop them sticking and burning.

3 Skim any scum from the top of the lentils using a spoon, then drain and rinse them thoroughly. Tip into a mixing bowl along with the onion, garlic and beetroot, and mash to a pulp. An ordinary jug blender, or any kind of food processor, will make this job easier, but it's not essential; a fork or masher and a good dollop of elbow grease will yield a pretty satisfying result, too.

Recipe continues overleaf

4 When it's a rough pulp, grate the bread into crumbs and mix through, with a pinch of salt and a good squeeze of lemon juice. Cover the mixture and chill it in the fridge for half an hour to firm up.

5 When firm to touch, preheat the oven to 180°C/350°F/gas 4. Shape the mixture into small balls and place them on a lightly greased baking tray. Drizzle the top with a little extra oil, or brush each one if you can be bothered, and bake in the centre of the oven for 25 minutes, turning over halfway through. And serve. I like mine with mayo (vegan, garlic), a generous helping of slaw, and a pile of little gramcakes (see page 68).

TIP

● At my local supermarket the fresh bunched beetroot is £1.80 for 500g, and the peeled and cooked vacuum-packed beets are 80p for 250g, so they actually work out cheaper. It seems illogical but I can only imagine they would be the smaller beets or those 'less pretty' than the big glorious ones that make it into the bunches. Which is speculation, but I'm applying Tinned Spud Theory and it makes sense. Anyway, it's a matter of personal preference and budget, but unless I'm seducing someone with a raw gorgeous salad (and let's face it, who even does that?!), I'll take the pre-cooked cheaper beets every time. They don't stain your fingers as much either.

RED BEAN SOUP AND DUMPLINGS

SERVES 4

1 large onion, diced

4 fat garlic cloves, minced

1 small red chilli, finely sliced, or a pinch of chilli flakes

oil, for frying

a pinch of ground allspice

1 large carrot or 2 smaller ones, diced

1 small potato, diced

1 sprig of thyme, leaves picked, or 1 tsp mixed dried herbs

1 litre chicken or vegetable stock (homemade or from a stock cube)

2 x 400g tins of kidney beans, drained and rinsed (about 500g drained weight)

2 rashers of bacon, to garnish

Regular readers will know that I am near-fanatical about the humble kidney bean, a throwback to the days when a 400g tin was 17p on the bottom shelves of the supermarket (now twice the price). I mashed them into burgers, used them to pad out chillies or plump up a goulash – my love for the little red bean knows no bounds.

One afternoon, sitting in the pub with my friend Chriss, I found a kindred kidney bean spirit. 'Red pea soup,' he announced, enthusiastically recounting holidays in Jamaica. Soup? Out of kidney beans? I was intrigued, and went rifling through cookbooks for recipe inspiration. And voilà, I wasn't disappointed. Traditional recipes use a base of pork bones and/or shredded beef, but I've gone for some bacon as a tasty addition instead. Deeply satisfying and simple to make, just don't skimp on the spinners (dumplings).

Recipe continues overleaf

FOR THE SPINNERS (DUMPLINGS)

100g plain flour

a pinch of salt and a bit of cracked black pepper

1 sprig of thyme, leaves picked, or 1 tsp mixed dried herbs

1 Toss the onion, garlic and chilli into a good-sized saucepan with a little oil and the allspice. Soften on low heat for a few minutes.

2 Add the carrot and potato – I scrub, rather than peel my veg – rumour has it that the best bits are lurking under the skin, so leave it on. Add the thyme or mixed herbs, pour over the stock and crank up the heat to bring it to the boil. Reduce to a simmer. Add the kidney beans to the pan, giving it all a good stir. While that does its thing, make your spinners.

3 Mix the flour, salt and thyme leaves or mixed herbs in a bowl with a good grind of pepper. Make a well (a sort of hole) in the middle and add 50–60ml water, mixing to form a stiff (but not dry and cracking) dough. With floured hands, form into small balls and drop into the soup.

4 Simmer for 15 minutes, until most of the kidney beans have broken down and thickened the soup, and the spinners are cooked through. Fry the bacon in a dry frying pan over high heat until super-crispy, smash it into pieces and scatter on top of each bowl of soup for extra salty deliciousness.

CONTRABAND

I started writing this cookery book before I gave up animal products, and so was faced with a small moral dilemma. Did I can these recipes for good, knowing that they could still be helpful to people on a bootstrap budget, or did I shove most of them all together in one chapter that my vegetarian readers can tape together, or tear out, or just flick past? I asked my readers and the overwhelming majority said that they didn't mind if they were included, so here they are. Tinned fish, chicken liver, turkey mince padded out with a can of beans – while it is true that eating meat will use up more of your weekly budget, there are a few tricks you can keep up your sleeve to make it go further. (If you do tear this chapter out, can you do it neatly, and consider donating it to your local food bank please to photocopy or hand out? Thank you very much.)

TURKEY BATMAN AND PLANES AND MORE

1 x 400g tin of haricot or cannellini beans, drained and rinsed

250g turkey mince

2 tbsp plain flour

1 medium egg

2 slices of bread (or use dried breadcrumbs)

a pinch of salt and a bit of cracked black pepper

a few pinches of fresh or dried herbs (optional)

1 tsp paprika (optional)

cooked peas, to serve (optional)

If you don't have a cookie cutter to hand, you can make these flat and round and they can be dinosaur toes! Any excess turkey mixture can be kept and frozen for meatballs, burgers or more turkey shapes … or roll it all and use it up, freezing any you don't want to cook.

1 Put the beans into a small saucepan and cover with water. Bring to the boil, then reduce to a simmer and cook for 5–10 minutes until tender. Drain the beans and tip into a mixing bowl, then mash to a pulp with the turkey mince. Stir in 1 tablespoon of flour to stiffen the mixture, and set to one side. If it is a warm day, pop it in the fridge. This helps it hold its shape.

2 Take two small bowls, while the turkey–bean mixture sets. Crack the egg into one and beat it well. Grate the bread into the other into crumbs. If you have a small blender, it is far less of a faff to just put the bread in that, in chunks, and pulse it into crumbs. At a pinch, dried breadcrumbs will do just fine. Season with salt and a little pepper. Add the herbs and paprika, if using.

3 Using the remaining flour, dust your hands lightly to prevent sticking, then form the turkey–bean mixture into balls. Around 1 tablespoon of mixture will make a decent-sized snack. Press each ball with your fingers until it is flat – around 1cm thick – and cut it into your desired shape with your cookie cutter. Tip the excess mixture back into the bowl. Dunk each shape in the egg, then roll in the breadcrumbs and place on a baking tray. (Now would be a good time to turn the oven on, at 180°C/350°F/gas 4, but don't put anything in it yet!)

4 Repeat until you have made as many as you want. Bake them in the oven for 20 minutes, turning once halfway through. And enjoy! Dunk them in ketchup – you've earned it. Serve with peas, if you like.

PRAWN AND SAUSAGE ETOUFFEE

SERVES 4

4 fat garlic cloves, finely minced

1 onion, finely sliced

1 pepper, any colour, deseeded and diced

a generous knob of butter

2 rounded tbsp plain flour

500ml chicken or fish stock, fresh or from a cube

1 level tbsp paprika

1 red chilli, chopped

4 sprigs of fresh thyme

6–8 sausages

1 x 400g tin of chopped tomatoes

300g prawns

a fistful of chopped fresh parsley

a pinch of salt and a bit of pepper, to taste

This was my first meal on landing in Los Angeles in the middle of the night a couple of years ago. All I wanted was my bed, clean crisp sheets to absorb the clammy stuffed-in feeling that only ten hours on an aeroplane can bring, but friends had asked us over for dinner. And what a comforting, restorative dinner it was! I was too shy to ask what it was or how to make it, but did some research on landing back in colder climes and came up with this. Dougie made his with shrimp and small smoked sausages, and the sauce was more golden than mine turns out, but this is a fairly good approximation of what happened that night. Serve with hot white rice and cold pale beer.

1 Toss the garlic, onion and pepper into a medium sauté pan with the butter on low heat. Cook low and slow for a few minutes until the veg start to soften. Add the flour and stir quickly to make a rough paste.

2 Add a little splash of stock to loosen, and stir again to smooth out any lumps. Repeat, adding stock to thin to a gravy consistency – not too thick and not too thin. The sauce will thicken as it heats through, so don't worry too much if you have a lot of stock left, you can add it later.

3 Stir in the paprika, chilli and thyme, and add the sausages and chopped tomatoes. Bring to the boil, reduce the heat and simmer for 20 minutes, stirring occasionally to disturb.

4 Remove from the heat, and stir in the prawns and parsley. Serve atop white fluffy rice, with extra butter, salt and pepper.

BBQ COLA RIBS

SERVES 4

4 fat garlic cloves, crushed

1 large onion, finely sliced

2 tbsp vegetable oil

a pinch of salt and a bit of cracked black pepper

1 x 400g tin of chopped tomatoes

2 tbsp tomato purée

½ tsp mustard (I like English, but any will do)

330ml can of full-sugar cola

500g pork ribs

Ribs are one of the cheapest cuts of pig, so back when I was a carnivore, I would make this dish as an occasional treat – it's not the healthiest recipe, since I use full-sugar cola for extra-sticky sweetness.

If you're a frugal foodie, scrub the bones clean to make a pork bone stock (the roasting will have brought out their flavour) – cover with water, bring to the boil and simmer them for a few hours on low heat with some garlic, carrot, onion, herbs and salt for a succulent slow-cooked stock.

1 **To make the ribs, toss the garlic and onion into a shallow pan with the oil. Season, and gently sauté over low heat for a few minutes to soften. Transfer the mix into a blender, add the chopped tomatoes, tomato purée and mustard and pulse to a rough liquid. Pour back into the saucepan – it might look a little messy right now, but trust me, it gets better. Add the can of cola and crank up the heat to bring to the boil, mixing well. Reduce the heat and simmer for 10 minutes to form a thick sauce that falls slowly from your spoon.**

2 **Preheat the oven to 180°C/350°F/gas 4. If you have a meat cleaver, halve your ribs to make them shorter – I like picking at smaller ribs, and so does my son. However, it's a numbers thing when you're feeding a horde, rather than a recipe necessity, so don't rush out to buy a butcher's chopper if you don't have one.**

3 **Line a roasting tray with foil. Pop the ribs in and cover with the sauce. Cover the tray loosely with more foil and cook in the centre of the oven for 1 hour. Whip off the foil, spoon the sauce back over and cook for a further half an hour. Enjoy.**

SARDINE AND TOMATO SOUP

SERVES 2

1 onion, finely sliced

1 x 120g tin of sardines in oil

1 x 400g tin of chopped tomatoes

1 tbsp (or more) lemon juice, fresh or bottled

a pinch of salt and a bit of cracked black pepper

In 2014, the Royal Court released a micro-play in collaboration with the *Guardian*, called *Britain Isn't Eating*. They interviewed me as part of the research, reading excerpts from my blog about the realities of being hungry and desperate in modern-day Britain. The actress Katherine Parkinson played a politician lecturing the poor on basic meals – but discovered that knocking together something nutritious and thrifty from the tins handed out at food banks wasn't as simple as she thought. Her 'dish' was a sardine and tomato soup, and as I watched the play, I wondered if these two ingredients, with a little culinary nouse, could actually become a decent, satisfying meal. This was the result – and I have served it to friends time and again to delight and acclaim. It needs a slow cook to break down the ostentatious fishiness of the sardines, so if you can't commit to half an hour on the hob, don't attempt it. Some gastronomic alchemy happens in the last 10 minutes of cooking. In its first incarnation, I tasted it 20 minutes in and despaired, threw a generous dash of lemon in and glowered at it for 10 more minutes, then something else emerged. I frequently hurl in a fistful of greens, a block of frozen spinach or a shake of peas for some bright green goodness. It can also serve as a cousin of the puttanesca, folded through spaghetti and topped with cheese.

1 Toss the onion into a saucepan. Peel open the tin of sardines and carefully pour the oil over the onion. Cook gently over medium heat for 5 minutes or so, stirring occasionally to stop the onions sticking and browning.

2 Pour in the tomatoes, followed by the sardines. The bones are generally soft enough to eat, but remove anything unusual if you have concerns. Flake the sardines with a fork and stir well into the tomatoes and onions.

3 Add 250ml water and the lemon juice, and turn up the heat. Bring to the boil, stirring occasionally, then reduce to a simmer for around half an hour, stirring. Stay close by and stir regularly to make sure it doesn't burn. You may need to add a dash more water as required.

4 When thickened and glossy, add lemon juice to taste to brighten and balance if the fish flavour is too strong. Season to taste, and serve.

HOT SARDINES WITH A HERBY SAUCE

SERVES 2

**a fistful of fresh
parsley or coriander
(or both, if you're
feeling fancy)**

**2 tbsp bottled lemon
juice**

a little black pepper

1 tbsp oil

**1 x 120g tin of
sardines in oil**

**a pinch of chilli flakes
(optional)**

Roasting sardines is a staple in my ancestry and that of many other Mediterranean cultures. I was sceptical when I first came across them in one of my great-aunt's cookbooks, but they quickly became a firm favourite, not just for their deliciousness, but because I could pick up two tins of sardines for less than £1 from most supermarkets – even the small corner-shop iterations.

For those of you who will forever associate sardines with disappointing school dinners, I have added a fresh and zingy sauce to counterbalance the salty, preserved flavour. Orange or lime work well in place of the lemon juice (bottled lemon is my bootstrap default), or a dash of vinegar will do.

1 Make your sauce – this is best combined in a jar with a lid to shake it all up, but a small bowl and a vigorous hand will do just fine. Finely chop the herbs, stalks and all, and place into a jar or bowl. Add the lemon juice, black pepper and oil, and mix vigorously. Taste it – it should be sharp and zingy. Leave it to stand to one side while you do the rest.

2 Peel back the lid of the tin of sardines and tip them, oil and all, into a frying pan. Put over high heat for a moment until they start to sizzle, then turn them over and cook the other side. Reduce the heat to medium and cook for a few more minutes to warm through.

3 Serve on toast, or atop a pile of mash, or with rice, and generously spoon the sauce on top. Finish with a pinch of chilli, if you like, and enjoy.

ANCHOVY SAVOURIES

SERVES 2, OR 1 IF
YOU'RE HUNGRY

1 tsp butter

1 tsp plain flour

120ml milk

**a lump of hard strong
cheese, to taste**

**a pinch of cayenne
pepper**

**4 slices of good
white bread**

**a fistful of fresh
chopped parsley**

**6 anchovies, fresh or
tinned in brine – the
choice is yours**

This may seem like the sort of simple thing you don't need a recipe for, more an idea than a prescriptive set of instructions. I stumbled across it in my copy of *Mrs Beeton's Everyday Cookery*, and as a bit of an anchovy fiend, I was immediately sold. The original calls for 'very thick white sauce and essence of anchovy'. I jotted it down in my notebook as one to explore. A few weeks later, I was having a light lunch at the Brackenbury, in Shepherd's Bush, run by Ossie, son of the late, great Rose Gray, and an anchovy toast savoury appeared from the kitchen. The notebook came back out (to the chagrin of anyone who accompanies me these days, I rarely have a meal without a pen in my hand). Under Mrs Beeton went Ossie Gray. Simple it may be, but if it's good enough for Isabella and Ossie, it's definitely good enough for me.

1 Make the cheese sauce. Gently melt the butter in a small saucepan on very low heat, and whisk in the flour with a fork to form a smooth paste. Add a splash of the milk and mix well, then keep gradually adding the milk, mixing all the time to stop lumps and clumps forming. If you get lumps, pop a sieve over a bowl and pour the mixture through to separate the lumps from the liquid. Tip the lumps back into the pan with a smattering of flour to recombine, add a little more butter, and start adding the liquid back in gradually. Things rarely go so wrong that they aren't redeemable.

2 Grate in the cheese, add the cayenne, give it all a stir and remove from the heat to settle and thicken.

3 Meanwhile, toast the bread until golden. Smear the cheese sauce on both pieces, add a smattering of chopped parsley, pop in the anchovies, and voilà! The sloppy sauce is part of the appeal for me, but you can firm up the whole experience with extra cheese, if you like.

BLACK PUDDING HASH

SERVES 4, MAKES
AROUND 10 FRITTERS

200g white potatoes

3 carrots

**1 large onion, finely
diced**

**a fistful of fresh
parsley, torn**

4 tbsp plain flour

1 egg

**400g black pudding,
diced**

oil, for frying

This is especially delicious (and healing) served with a couple of soft-boiled eggs and some lightly fried bread.

1 Line a colander with kitchen roll or a clean, non-fluffy tea towel, and grate in the potatoes and carrots – potatoes first, as they tend to be wetter, so the weight of the carrots will bear down on them. Squish the excess water out by pushing down on the grated veg.

2 Tip the grated veg into a bowl, then add the onion and parsley, stir in the flour and egg, then stir in the black pudding. Cover and chill for at least half an hour – this helps the mixture bind together and stops it falling apart in the pan.

3 Heat a little oil in a frying pan, dollop in a tablespoon of the mixture, flatten it slightly and fry on medium–high heat for a few minutes on each side. Repeat with the remaining mixture until it is all used up.

SOUTHERN FRIED LIVERS

SERVES 4

150g flour (self-raising is best for a light batter)

¼ tsp sweet paprika

a pinch of salt and a bit of cracked black pepper

150ml whole milk, plus extra for the livers (optional)

500g chicken livers and/or thighs (depending on your family's tastes)

oil, for frying

Liver is cheap, lean, rich in iron and vitamins and general goodness, and takes minutes to prepare and cook. My child, however, is yet to be convinced. I've just about got away with a liver Bolognese and a pâté or two, but I once tried a mix of chicken thighs and livers, battered and deep-fried; the white meat for him and the offal for me. He dunked the livers in ketchup along with the white meat nuggets, and didn't say a word …

1 **For best results, make the batter an hour ahead, cover and leave it in the fridge – the lightest, crispest batters are achieved by very cold batter hitting hot, hot oil. Combine the flour, paprika, salt and pepper; whisk in a little of the milk to a smooth paste, then gradually add more until you have a smooth and runny batter. Cover and chill.**

2 **Pop the livers in a bowl with a little milk to soak, cover and put them in the fridge alongside the batter.**

3 **When the batter is nice and cold, thinly slice the chicken livers and thighs and set to one side – they're going to be cooked briefly in hot oil, so if left too chunky, they might not cook through.**

4 **Heat the oil in a small saucepan until it is gently bubbling. Turn down the heat and drop in a small amount of batter. If it fizzes and floats to the top, all golden and crispy, you're ready to go. Dip each piece of liver and chicken into the batter, fry for around 6 minutes until cooked through, remove and place on a piece of kitchen roll or a clean tea towel to drain the excess oil.**

5 **Repeat until all the liver and thigh is used. Cut one open to check it is cooked through. If you are in any doubt as to whether your chicken is fully cooked, bake it at 180°C/350°F/gas 4 for 15 minutes. Serve piping hot!**

DAD'S CHINESE CHICKEN CURRY

SERVES 4

4 tbsp vegetable oil

1 large onion, sliced

chunk of fresh root ginger, peeled and finely chopped

4 fat garlic cloves, finely chopped

1 small red chilli, finely chopped

a pinch of salt and a bit of cracked black pepper

2 tsp plain flour

1 tsp turmeric

1 tsp cumin, seeds or ground

1 tsp ground coriander

1 chicken stock cube dissolved in 500ml boiling water

3 chicken thighs

3 chicken drumsticks

100g frozen peas

Dinners at my parents' house were always eaten at the table, but often, half an hour beforehand, extra settings were hurriedly assembled. They were foster carers, and unexpected new arrivals meant meals were usually prepared in bulk – if no extras were needed, the leftovers made a welcome lunch the next day. One of my fondest memories is of my father presenting us with an exact replica of a chicken curry from the local Chinese restaurant, complete with mustard-yellow sauce and studded with green peas. This is a tribute to his take on theirs – although I add garlic to mine, which he can't stand. Sorry, Dad.

1 Gently heat half the oil in a medium pan. Add the onion, ginger, garlic and chilli (discard the seeds if you don't like too much heat). Season and cook over low, slow heat for a few minutes. Add the flour and spices, and stir well. When the onion is coated in the flour and spices, add a splash of stock and stir well to form a rough paste. Add a splash more stock to thin and stir through for a minute.

2 Remove from the heat and blitz to a paste in a blender or food processor. Return to the heat and continue to add the stock, stirring vigorously to prevent lumps. Set to one side.

3 Add the rest of the oil to a new pan and cook the chicken over high heat, turning it to seal the edges. Pour over the sauce, bring to the boil, cover, reduce to a simmer and cook for 30 minutes, until it has thickened and the chicken is cooked through. Stir occasionally, and add more water if needed. Add the peas a few minutes before serving.

EAT MORE GREENS

Eating veg when you're on a shoestring budget can be a challenge. I base my recipes around supermarket freezer or tinned aisles with the idea that most people have one within reasonable distance, but have a poke around your local area for small independent shops too, as they are often cheaper, and have some wildly exciting bits and pieces kicking around. Frozen peas and spinach are hugely useful for the financially straitened cook, and I often fling a handful of either into whatever I'm cooking. Feel free to substitute fresh greens if you have them. Fresh cabbage is seemingly unfashionable these days, but the nobbly-rough texture of Savoy is ideal finely sliced, gently cooked and tossed through pasta, to scoop up any lingering sauces. Greens are fairly interchangeable, so you can mix these up with kale, spinach, cabbage, spring greens, peas, even finely sliced lettuce. Go wild, go on. Once you start hurling fistfuls of vegetation around, you may not be able to stop.

MUSHROOM ROGAN JOSH (VE)

SERVES 2

2 medium-sized onions or 1 massive one, finely sliced

4 fat garlic cloves, smashed or finely chopped (see Tip)

4 cardamom pods

2 tbsp oil

1 tsp ground coriander (dhaniya powder)

½ tsp turmeric

a few pinches of ground cinnamon

a pinch of salt and a bit of cracked black pepper, to taste

a few pinches of chilli flakes, to taste

200g mushrooms, sliced

1 x 400g tin of chopped tomatoes

dash of lemon juice (optional)

a fistful of fresh coriander or parsley, to finish

50ml coconut cream/ full-fat coconut milk/ coconut yoghurt/ coconut cream – you get the drift (optional)

Last night I fancied a curry; a nice hot curry to warm the very cockles of my draughty flat, but like so many evenings of 'cooking for one', I just couldn't decide which one to have. I opened the fridge, glowered at a bunch of onions and a handful of mushrooms, and took to Twitter with a poll. It's my new favourite way of, to coin a phrase, Making Your Mind Up. (I challenge you, Brits of a certain age, to not take that on as an earworm now. I make no apologies.)

The poll returned me a mushroom rogan josh over a korma or vindaloo, and I set about making it. I find cooking for one such an indulgent pleasure, such a selfish moment, a treat. Those of you who follow me on Instagram will have noticed I often cook very late at night, when the boy-child is sleeping, when the last emails have been answered, when peace has been restored to my chaotic home, I stand over my hob and delight in the selfish pleasure of satisfying my senses, one by one by one . . . I digress. Mushroom rogan josh recipes online vary wildly, from the eyebrow-raising 'take a jar of madras paste' on the BBC Good Food website, to paprika, to Jamie Oliver's cloves and allsorts. I picked all the bits I liked from about seven different recipes, made it vegan, adjusted it to taste as I went along, and when done, carried the pan to bed and devoured the lot. The coconut cream, etc, is not essential but it is good for tempering the spice if you are cooking for young mouths or people with less of a tolerance for the hot stuff. Non-vegans can replace this with natural yoghurt.

Here's my mushroom rogan josh, so delicious that I had it cold for breakfast, smeared on toast with a fistful of spinach, too.

1 Throw the onions and garlic into a pan. Break the cardamom pods (see garlic method in Tip, or carefully halve them with a sharp knife) and release the seeds into the pan. If you don't have cardamom, a just-as-good substitute would be star anise, fennel seed or caraway, but just a little.

2 Add the oil and warm the pan through over medium heat. Stir to disturb and stop the onions from burning, and inhale as the cardamom seeds toast, pop and release their delicate, heady fragrance. You deserve this. Love yourself. Treat yourself. Enjoy.

3 Give it all a few minutes, and when the onion starts to soften, add the remaining spices. In goes the coriander, turmeric, cinnamon, a pinch of salt, a crack of pepper and chilli flakes with a stir. Toss in the mushrooms, coat them in the spices, and let those, too, soften for a moment.

4 Pour over the tomatoes, add 150ml water, and stir. Bring to a bubbling boil, then reduce to a simmer. Cook until the sauce has thickened, around 20 minutes, and then taste it. Add salt if you like it and a dash of lemon juice to brighten it, if you wish. Serve with coriander or parsley and a dollop of coconut cream or your preferred equivalent, on top.

TIPS

● This has a relatively long cooking time for one of my recipes, so you can just lay the garlic on the worktop, place the fattest knife you have flat across it, and firmly drive the heel of your palm down to crush it. Please be careful. Please don't drive your palm into the sharp bit. Please chop it in a regular fashion if you have any concerns about this. Finding a soft, creamy, still-slightly-pungent broken clove of garlic in my dinner is one of my favourite foodie delights, but if you feel differently about this, chop it up finely.

● If you're cooking rice with this, for what it's worth, I cook my rice with a few pinches of turmeric, cinnamon and a fistful of sultanas. Sometimes I add a cardamom pod or star anise or two, sometimes stir through coconut milk or cream at the end to make a sticky kind-of-pilau-risotto. Sometimes it takes a bunch of spinach, parsley or coriander for colour and goodness, other times I leave it yellow and glorious.

UMAMI MUSHROOMS (V)

SERVES 2

30g dried mushrooms

1 small onion, finely sliced

a pinch of salt

2 fat garlic cloves, roughly chopped

1 tbsp oil or butter

100g fresh mushrooms, sliced or torn

1 tbsp dark soy sauce

This recipe seems and sounds too simple to be true, but sometimes the best dishes are those that allow their ingredients to sing at the tops of their voices without too much complicated fannying around drowning them out. I love a mushroom, especially when I can find exotic varieties reduced to clear in the corner shops and supermarkets, taking them home and drying them out low and slow in the bottom of the oven to use again at a later date.

It is these dried mushrooms that make up the mushroom stock in this recipe, but if you don't have any, just cook fresh ones for a little longer than the recipe suggests. These pair perfectly with a pile of buttery mashed potato, or fried rice, or my Moonshine Mash (see page 145).

1 Make a mushroom stock by popping the dried mushrooms in a saucepan and covering with a little water.

2 Toss in half the onion along with a pinch of salt. Bring to the boil then reduce to a simmer for 30 minutes, until the liquid is rich and dark and ominous-looking. You may need to top up the water periodically to stop it from all evaporating away, which would be a terrible shame! When the stock is ready, remove from the heat and pour it into a mug or jug, and set to one side.

3 Toss the garlic and the remaining onion into the now-empty saucepan with the oil or butter. Don't worry about cleaning the pan, any lingering flavours from the stock will only enhance this step. Add the mushrooms, too. Cook on medium heat for a few minutes until the vegetables start to soften, then pour over the stock. Bring back to the boil, and reduce to a simmer for a few minutes more. Finish by stirring through the soy sauce, then serve.

BOLDSLAW (V)

SERVES 4 AS A SIDE

raw beetroot

carrots

red cabbage

spring onions (or ordinary)

kale or hispi cabbage

3 tbsp vinegar (any clear, not balsamic)

1 tsp salt

1 tbsp sugar

6 tbsp salad cream

10 tbsp mayo

fresh chopped herbs (mint, chives, parsley or coriander), to serve

Made for many a family barbecue, this is so-named for its bold colours and punchy flavour. Ordinary, mellow, creamy slaw be damned. Use as much or as little of each of the main ingredients as you like, or have to hand, but I tend to go with 'a generous fistful of everything'. (Pictured on previous page.)

1 Grate the beetroot and carrots and finely slice the red cabbage and onions. Roughly chop the kale or hispi cabbage. Toss everything into a bowl.

2 Macerate your vegetables – which means to soften by soaking in a liquid; in this case, vinegar, with the rough grains of salt and sugar helping to break them down. Mix well with clean hands to cover everything, cover the bowl and set to one side for at least half an hour.

3 Mix in the salad cream and mayo (just mayo will do at a push if you don't generally have salad cream in). The beets should turn everything a glorious pinky-purple colour.

4 Serve topped with fresh chopped herbs for a colour-contrasting wow factor (or don't bother if that sort of thing isn't important to you!). It can be kept in the fridge for up to 3 days; if it starts to separate, just give it a good stir before serving.

MUSHROOM AND SPINACH BOLOGNESE (V)

SERVES 2 ADULTS
AND 2 CHILDREN –
OR 3 ADULTS, OR 2
SERIOUSLY HUNGRY
ADULTS WHO DON'T
WANT TO MOVE FOR
THE REST OF THE
EVENING

**200–250g spaghetti
or pasta, depending
on above scenario**

**1 large onion, finely
sliced**

**4 fat garlic cloves,
finely sliced**

**250g mushrooms,
minced (see intro)**

2 tbsp oil

**a pinch of salt and a
bit of cracked black
pepper**

**4 tbsp tomato purée
or 1 x 400g tin of
chopped tomatoes**

**1 tbsp bottled lemon
juice, or dash of any
vinegar (optional)**

**100g frozen spinach
(or fresh)**

**1 tsp basic mixed
dried herbs**

**grated cheese or
vegan alternative,
to serve**

I've been meaning to share my 'mushroom mince' for ages – I use it instead of soya mince or Quorn as a cheaper alternative that isn't full of unpronounceable ingredients or a gazillion processes. It's simple, quick and actually tastes like food, and can be dried out and stored in a jar for months, or frozen to use as required.

Basically, finely slice some mushrooms, then chop them up like billy-o until they're finely diced. They'll shrink a bit in the pan as they lose moisture anyway. Then either use them straight away, or freeze, or spread thinly on a baking tray (or any tray) on a layer of kitchen roll and leave to dry for a day or two somewhere safe and not moist (not the bathroom, for example).

Now for the fun part – a Bolognese packed full of veg, costing pennies, suitable for your vegan friends but convincing enough for the carnivores – enjoy! This is my new favourite winter comforting bowl-food.

1 Bring a pan of water to the boil, then toss the pasta into the pan, reduce the heat and cook according to the packet instructions, usually simmering for 8–10 minutes, or until cooked.

2 While the pasta is cooking, toss the onion, garlic and mushroom mince into a pan with the oil, salt and pepper and turn the heat up high for a minute or two, taking care not to burn anything by stirring well to disturb it. Turn the heat down to low–medium, depending what hob ring you have it on, then add all remaining ingredients and stir well. Bring back to high heat, add half a small cup of water (about 125ml) to loosen the tomato purée, stir well to combine and reduce the heat, stirring occasionally.

3 When the pasta is cooked, your Bolognese should look – well, like a Bolognese. Taste it – and season as required. It may need a dash more lemon juice or a smudge of vinegar, or a pinch of salt, or a smattering more herbs – it's up to you. And enjoy! If you aren't a vegan, top with cheese as you normally would, if you are, then you probably know of good vegan cheese alternatives already.

KALE, CHICKPEA AND PEANUT CURRY (V)

SERVES 2

1 large onion, finely sliced

2 fat garlic cloves, chopped (optional, works fine without)

1 tbsp oil

1 tbsp cumin, seeds or ground

1 tsp turmeric powder

⅛ tsp mustard seeds or actual mustard

1 x 400g tin of chickpeas, drained and rinsed

a handful or two of unsalted peanuts (or other nut, or sunflower seeds if allergic to nuts)

1 x 400g tin of chopped tomatoes

a fistful of kale or other greens

zest and juice of ½ lemon, or 1–2 tbsp bottled lemon juice

a pinch of salt and a bit of pepper, to taste

a pinch of chilli flakes, to serve

natural yoghurt or a splash of milk, to serve (to temper heat if feeding to kids)

I use kale for this recipe as it is cheap to buy from the supermarket or greengrocers, despite its insurgence a few years back as a trendy superfood. It's true that it is good for you, I mean, it's green and leafy and as a rule the green leafy (edible!) things tend to be packed full of vitamins and nutrients, but I shan't bore you with the pseudobabble about why you should be eating it, because, presumably, that's not what you or I are here for. If kale isn't to your liking or you can't get hold of it, any other leafy green will do as a fine substitute. Try spring greens, spinach, gnarly Savoy cabbage, or anything that takes your fancy.

This recipe is quick and simple, and I often make a batch of it, as it is great in sandwiches, pittas or wraps the next day, or slung in the freezer for a ready meal for the future, because, let's face it, we all have days where slinging something in the microwave is about all we can be bothered with. Even me. I portion it up before I sit down to eat mine, else I would just carry on noshing it from the pan and the good intentions about eating leftovers would be a fond memory. Besides, then I can bung the pan in the sink and by the time we've finished dinner, it's all but washed itself. It's the small things.

1 Put the onion and garlic into a largish pan. Add the oil, cumin, turmeric and mustard and gently soften over low heat. Don't be tempted to crank up the heat as you may burn the spices and onions. Chargrilled onions have a wonderful flavour all of their own, reminiscent of hot dogs and school fayres and childhood football matches, but they don't belong here, I'm afraid. Stir the pan occasionally to disturb everything, to prevent it sticking and browning.

2 Toss the chickpeas in with the nuts/seeds, tomatoes, greens and a splash of water. Now turn the heat up full and stir all together until bubbling, then reduce the heat to low and cook for at least 20 minutes, until the sauce has thickened and reduced. The longer this cooks, the better it gets, so you can carry on for up to an hour if your budget permits it (see Tip below).

3 For the benefit of the long slow cook without the hour-long gas usage, you can crank it up to piping hot, remove from the heat, cover with tin foil or a lid or large plate, and wrap the whole thing in a large fluffy towel or dressing gown and leave it to cool. Wrapping it up will insulate some of the heat, and it will continue to cook as it cools. Leave it for the hour, and heat through to serve.

4 However you end up cooking it – for 20 minutes, for an hour, or wrapped in a bathrobe, heat it back through to serve, add the lemon zest and juice, salt and pepper, and stir well. Dress with chilli flakes and serve with natural yoghurt, if you like.

TIP

• All energy tariffs are confusingly different, as are all ovens, hobs, pans, kitchens, but as a rough guide, when I was on a key card gas meter in 2016, running my large hob for an hour cost around 6p. Filling my bath was 45p, whereas a quick morning shower was 8p. I kept a record as and when I remembered, out of curiosity, but there are too many variables to confidently guess what it would cost an average household.

BROCCOLI AND COURGETTE 'PESTO' (V)

SERVES 2

100g broccoli, stems and all, finely chopped

2 garlic cloves

250g courgette, finely chopped

50g spinach, fresh or frozen and defrosted

100g bread, stale or otherwise, torn

100ml oil

30ml lemon juice, bottled is fine

a pinch of salt

strong grated cheese, to serve (for non-vegans), but it's perfectly delicious the way it is

This recipe is made with bread to give it that nutty texture that's so great about pesto, without any actual nuts. I like to freeze it – up to you whether to refreeze it if using defrosted spinach, I've been doing it for years with veg and never caught vegetable lurgies, but health and safety scaremongerers abound.

You can play with the vegetables, and veg proportions – I just include enough broccoli to pass mine off as 'broccoli sauce' – and Small Boy is none the wiser. Hoorah for a penchant for pesto, in my household at least …

1 Put the broccoli, garlic, courgette, spinach and bread in the blender – pulse until it resembles a pesto. The wetness of the courgette should help it along, but if your blender is struggling, add the oil and lemon juice, and if it's still struggling, a small slosh of water. The breadcrumbs will soak the liquid up anyway.

2 Stir through the salt and the cheese and divide the pesto among small jars or containers and store one in the fridge and one in the freezer for a cheat dinner at a later date. Serve over hot pasta, and enjoy.

TIP

● If you're seriously suspicious about your kids eating 'raw' veg, you can tip this into a pan and cook it off for a few minutes before tipping it over their pasta – but I find a good grating of cheese goes a long way in getting kids to eat anything (vegan cheese for vegans, obviously, and not so much for everyone else).

SELF-LOVE STEW

SERVES 1

oil, for frying

2 garlic cloves, roughly chopped

1 onion, roughly chopped

a few handfuls of finely chopped or grated root veg (I like carrot, parsnip, spud, sweet potato – any root will do)

1 tsp paprika

150g tofu or 2 white fish fillets

1 x 400g tin of beans (baked, kidney, butter, cannellini, chickpeas – any beans), drained

1 x 400g tin of chopped tomatoes

a fistful of kale or spinach

a squeeze of lemon juice

a pinch of salt and a bit of cracked black pepper

This recipe first appeared on my Instagram account (for readers clutching this book in a post-apocalyptic wasteland, Instagram is a photograph-sharing network where people mostly show off their dinner and houses that are much larger and cleaner than mine). It was a rough night, in the middle of a tough week, embedded in a hellish year, and I wasn't cooking. Overwhelmed by life and sadness, I hadn't been in my kitchen for days. I needed comfort, and nourishment, and I forced myself to the stove. This revelation may come as something of a surprise, but even I can't cook sometimes. This did the trick – and you can use a handful of frozen veg in place of chopping anything, if you like. (Pictured overleaf.)

1 Warm a little oil in a pan over low heat and cook the garlic and onion to soften. Stir, stir, slow and cathartic.

2 Add the finely chopped or grated root veg and stir some more, then add the paprika and stir in. The stirring is key. It is soothing. It is mindless, not mindful. Sod mindful. My mind is full enough. It is a minefield. Sometimes I want to stir some stuff and stare at my hands or into nothing.

3 Chuck in some chunks of tofu if you're veggie/vegan, or white or tinned fish if you aren't. Tip in the beans. Whatever beans – add them for goodness. For laziness. For filling comfort. For making it stretch into an extra meal you won't have to cook. Pour over the tomatoes. The cheaper ones are brilliantly sloppy and liquid and excellent for soups and stews.

4 Shred some kale in your hands. Rip it the heck up with all the stress and physicality you can muster. Go on. Tear it to shreds. Drop it in. Stir it through, breathe, and stir, and breathe.

5 Bring to the boil, like your fury, heat it up and watch it roar … then reduce it to a simmer. Douse in lemon juice to brighten, add some salt and pepper to amplify the flavours.

♥

Spoon it into a bowl.

Sit in your favourite spot.

Hug that bowl to yourself.

Enjoy every mouthful.

Shoulders down.

You did this.

You made this for yourself out of love.

You are nourishing yourself.

You are smart.

You are kind to yourself.

You are important.

And you can wash up tomorrow.

TOFU SHASHLIK (VE)

SERVES 2–3 AS PART
OF A MAIN MEAL

**1 small onion, finely
sliced**

**4 fat garlic cloves,
roughly chopped**

**a small piece of
fresh root ginger,
roughly chopped
(not essential)**

2 tbsp oil

**1 tsp ground
coriander**

**1 tsp cumin, seeds
or ground**

**a pinch or two of
chilli flakes**

**1 x 400g tin of
chopped tomatoes**

**100g peppers,
chopped**

200g frozen spinach

**100g firm tofu,
drained (see Tip)
and diced**

2 tsp any flour

a few pinches of salt

**100g frozen peas,
or a handful of
greens (optional)**

Take-aways generally have a fairly decent range for herbivores, but I often find myself hankering after a shashlik. Shashlik is usually skewered meat cooked in spices before being blasted in a tandoor oven, and having neither a tandoor nor any inclination to nibble on a duck or a lamb, I started to ponder how I could make a reasonably authentic veggie version. Mushrooms were out, aubergine would probably be okay, but wasn't quite what I wanted, and then I landed on the reduced tofu in the supermarket. Bingo. The tofu shashlik was born. I posted it on Twitter and hundreds of you asked for the recipe, so here it is.

1 Toss the onion, garlic and ginger into a saucepan with a splash of the oil. Add the spices and cook on medium heat for a few minutes to start to soften. Pour in the tomatoes and add the peppers and spinach, stir well, and transfer to a back burner on low heat to cook. This forms the sauce for the shashlik and will benefit from the longest possible cooking time you can bear to give it. I do mine for around an hour, but not everyone's budgets and patience will stretch to that, so 15 minutes is just fine.

2 When the sauce is thickened and smells delicious, you can start to cook the tofu.

3 Pop it in a bowl with the flour and a pinch of salt. Give it a shake to coat it and slightly rough up the edges – this is important for the crisp factor, as dishevelled edges cook faster than clean and tidy Stepford Wives ones. This is the secret to perfect roast potatoes, too – to throw them around a bit.

Recipe continues overleaf

4 Gently grease a frying pan with a little of the oil and pop over high heat to warm it, then carefully add the tofu. Cook for 3–4 minutes, then turn the tofu over to cook it on the other side. A cube has six sides, remember, so there is going to be some serious turning over to do if you are determined to have the crispiest tofu in all the land. When it is as crisp as you like, remove it and pop it in the pan of sauce sitting on the back of the stove.

5 Give it a quick stir and stir through the peas or greens, if you are cooking it for someone special (that can be you, you are special).

TIP

● When I first posted about this recipe, I was inundated with requests from people, especially about how to make tofu crispy. I'm no expert, as it is a new ingredient to me, but have just about managed to pull it off by now. First you make sure all of the excess water is gently squeezed out, similar to how you would gently squeeze a mozzarella ball or similar. I do this one of two ways – either place it in a sieve over the sink with a side plate over the top, and pop a tin or two of beans on top of the plate. The weighted pressure pushes the liquid out of the tofu and down the sink (in the interests of improved frugality, if anyone has a use for this, I am all ears). Or, I wrap it several times in a clean flat tea towel and gently press it between my hands over the sink, where the tea towel will absorb a good deal of the liquid. Either way, use 'firm' tofu, and give it a squish.

MUSHROOM AND TEA BOURGIGNON (VE)

SERVES 4

1 tea bag

300ml boiling water

1 medium onion (mine weighed 200g, but don't worry too much), finely sliced (see Tip)

4 fat garlic cloves, finely sliced

2 tbsp oil

a pinch of salt and a bit of cracked black pepper

1 x 400g tin of chopped tomatoes

2 tbsp tomato purée (optional but I like a nice tomatoey taste)

1 tsp mixed dried herbs

400g mushrooms, sliced

fistfuls of spinach, steamed, to serve (optional)

Now don't freak out, but here's a recipe for tea bourgignon. Like bourgignon for tea, but a little more exciting. The pedant in me thinks I can't exactly get away with calling this vegan heap of deliciousness a 'bourgignon', given that it doesn't have any beef or wine in it, but the rebel in me is shrugging her shoulders and recalling the hundreds of recipes I've cooked so far on this journey that deviate deliciously from their traditions and origins, and besides, 'mushroom stew' just doesn't have the same oh-no-she-didn't ring to it.

For a while now some of my readers have been asking what they can replace wine with in my recipes; either they don't have it, or it's too much of an outlay to go and buy a bottle just to use a splash here and there (and if anyone understands that, I do!). Well, my science head said one day that maybe strong black tea would give the same effect, and then by happy coincidence someone suggested it on one of my recipes a few days later and sealed the deal.

Recipe continues overleaf

1 Find the largest mug you have. Pop a tea bag in, and fill it with the boiling water. Let it stand to one side to stew, properly stew, while you do the next bits.

2 Toss the onion and garlic into a large pan. Pour the oil over, stir, add a pinch of salt and pop over medium heat. Cook for a few minutes, stirring occasionally, to soften the onions and lose that raw acerbic edge to them.

3 Pour over the chopped tomatoes and stir in the purée, and add the herbs. Remove the tea bag from the mug and pour the strong black tea into the pan, and give everything a stir. Toss in the mushrooms, then bring it all to the boil. Once boiling, reduce to a simmer and cook for at least 20 minutes to let the sauce reduce and thicken and all the flavours meld together in a super-delicious way.

4 The next bit is up to you. You can leave it simmering away for another half an hour in the traditional fashion, or you can turn the heat off, pop a lid on (or large plate or tin foil if you don't have a lid) and let it slowly cool down. It will carry on cooking itself with the heat trapped inside, but will cost you less in gas or electricity to achieve pretty much the same effect – it just won't reduce as much, so you'll need to strain some of the liquid off to serve, or eat it like a soup, which is equally yummy.

5 Season to taste, and serve. I like mine slopped onto white fluffy rice or a pile of mash, but if you're a low-carb person, a pile of spinach or steamed greens would be yummy too.

TIPS

• When one of my friends taught me to make curries many moons ago, he told me to chop the onions so finely that eventually they melt into the sauce with a long, slow cook; it's a principle I apply to most stews these days. Your onions might not vanish, but that's okay, too, mine don't always. Not all onions are created equal.

• To make it go further, you could sling a tin of cannellini beans (or rinsed-off baked beans) into it when you put the mushrooms in, which adds a hit of protein too, for people who worry about that sort of thing.

GREEN JUICE WITHOUT A JUICER (VE)

MAKES 300ML
STRONG JUICE,
SERVES 1 HARDENED
JUICE FIEND OR
2 GENTLER SOULS,
IF DILUTED

1 apple

a small slice of fresh root ginger

a handful of kale, or fresh or frozen (defrosted) spinach

1 celery stalk

½ lemon or 1 tbsp bottled lemon juice

When I'm down, or life goes a bit wrong, I retreat from the kitchen – I find it very hard to cook or be creative or even taste things properly when my head is off-balance. And so I mostly eat toast. Marmite on toast, leftovers on toast, something quick and mindless.

One afternoon last winter I figured enough was enough and my body was SCREAMING at me for fruit and vegetables – I've learned to listen to it over the years as those cravings are usually important. Anyway, unusually for us, the fruit bowl and veg drawer were seriously lacking, apart from a very bruised and squashy apple, a practically dry lemon, a wilted few stalks of celery and half a bag of kale I bought nearly a month ago that refuses to die. Unsurprisingly, I didn't want to eat any of it in its current pathetic state, so green juice it was. And it was a good opportunity to do something I've been meaning to do for a while now; a 'how to make juice without a juicer' recipe. You can use this method for practically any juice recipe that is already out there, or you can use it for my green juice, which despite its sorrowful origin is actually quite yummy. I usually have cucumber in place of the celery, but not today.

1 First dice everything up really small – don't worry about peeling the lemon or ginger, or deseeding anything. Since the whole 'NutriBullet' craze kicked off (basically throwing whole fruits and veggies into a tiny powerful expensive blender to pulverise them into a smoothie), I've been a lot more relaxed about peeling and deseeding things for juices. And by 'a lot more relaxed' I mean 'celebrated the excuse to be even more lazy – sorry, time-saving – in the kitchen'. So dice it all up, and pop it into a blender.

2 Add about 200ml water and blend until it is well combined. Pour into a sieve and hold over a bowl to catch the juice. If you don't have a sieve, line the bowl with a clean tea towel (not the microfibre sort or you run the risk of fluffy juice), pour the mix into it and gather the edges together. Hold it over the bowl and squeeze gently and the juice will pass through. Use a spoon to stir the pulp to get as much juice out as possible, and keep going – you'll be amazed at how much comes out with a vigorous stir. And voilà. Juice.

TIP

● If you're looking at that pulp and thinking it's a waste, it's about the same as you'd scrape out of your juicer. I put mine into ice cube trays and feed them to my guinea pig as treats. Some people add water again to the pulp and re-blend it for a second run at the juice, albeit a bit of a weaker version. Up to you. Still, now you can join the juicing craze without shelling out a hundred quid for a fashionable juicer.

SWEETS AND TREATS

Sometimes, on a glum day, there's nothing like a freshly baked cake to warm your kitchen and your cockles. Even if that cake is a microwave mug cake, or made from half a jar of jam and some old, slightly dubious flour. Dessert doesn't have to mean lavish, indulgent treats; as a child my favourite pudding was my Dad's trifle, which was pretty much a tin of fruit cocktail, jelly, and a can of Smartprice custard dumped on top. The fruit cocktail was 14p, the jelly 9p, and the custard around 9p too. The apple doesn't rock very far from the tree in our house, but when it did, it was turned into crumble . . .

TWO-INGREDIENT COCONUT HOT CHOCOLATE (VE)

MAKES
8–10 PORTIONS

100g dark chocolate

**100g coconut cream
(about ½ carton, or
add it all if you like
your chocolate sweet
and creamy)**

The idea for this came after midnight on a very cold November evening. At the time of first writing this recipe, I slept on a sofa bed in a bay beneath a set of single-glazed louvre windows – you know, the kind with the slats that overlap but don't quite meet. Which means that when the temperature drops, my goodness I know about it. I'm not complaining, though, as I love my small, beautiful, idiosyncratic home; it just means that one of the last things I do of an evening is curl into bed with the hottest drink imaginable and burrow under my duvet. And so, with no milk in the house of any kind, but half a block of coconut cream in the cupboard, this was born. I made a big batch, seeing that the weather was only going to get colder, and it's good to be prepared for this sort of thing. And it's vegan, too.

1 Take the smallest saucepan you have and fill with barely 5cm water. Balance a heatproof mixing bowl over the top, and bring the water to the boil over high heat. Take the bowl off and check the bottom; if it's wet, tip a little water out. It's important that the water doesn't touch the bowl, as according to great cookbooks and master chocolatiers, the melting chocolate becomes bitter.

2 Break up the chocolate and add it to the bowl, then reduce the heat to medium. Stir as the chocolate melts. If it starts to split (usually because water has touched the bottom of the bowl and scorched your poor choccy), simply add a splash of water and mix vigorously to bring it back together.

3 When the chocolate has all melted, add the coconut cream and around 150ml water. Give it a good stir to combine.

4 Portion the mixture into an ice cube tray for anytime-ready hot chocolate. To use, simply pop one out and melt on low–medium heat for a minute in the microwave. Add a splash of boiling water and stir well to loosen to a thick paste, repeat, and then top up your mug. For big mugs you may want to use two cubes, and if you really fancy a treat, top up with warm milk of your choice, but then it's a 3-ingredient hot chocolate. But I'll forgive you.

NOT-TOO-CHOCOLATEY CHOCOLATE AND BANANA CAKE (VE)

SERVES 8ISH

100g dark chocolate

75ml oil, plus extra for greasing

3 large, overripe bananas

50g granulated sugar, or more to taste

225g plain flour

2 tsp bicarbonate of soda

2 tbsp cocoa powder (optional)

Before the chocolate lovers perusing these pages recoil in horror at the idea of a chocolate cake any less than overwhelmingly dark and rich and sumptuous, let me reassure you that you can simply add 2 tablespoons of cocoa powder to this recipe to deepen it and satisfy your chocolate-craving tastebuds. For the rest of us, here's a (not-too-chocolatey) chocolate cake recipe. Oh, and it just so happens to be vegan, too. If bananas aren't your thing, substitute them with 4 tablespoons of apple sauce instead. You know, the kind you might buy at Christmas that then lurks in the back of the fridge for the next year until you buy another jar the next year.

1 **Preheat the oven to 160°C/325°F/gas 3 and lightly grease a 900g/2lb loaf or 20cm cake tin.**

2 **Pop barely 5cm water into a saucepan and balance a heatproof mixing bowl on top. Take the bowl off and check the bottom; if it's wet, tip a little water out. It's important that the water doesn't touch the bowl, as according to great cookbooks and master chocolatiers, the melting chocolate becomes bitter. Pop the lot onto a high heat and bring the water to the boil, then lower the heat so the water is simmering. Break up the chocolate and add it to the bowl with the oil, and stir as it starts to melt.**

3 **Meanwhile, in a separate bowl, peel the bananas and mash them to smithereens. The side of a teaspoon is an excellent, if unlikely, tool for the job, but a sturdy fork or wooden spoon will also do the trick.**

4 **When the chocolate has melted and is well mixed together, carefully remove from the heat. Stir in the banana mash, sugar, flour, bicarbonate of soda and cocoa powder, if using, and beat well to make your cake batter. Depending on how ripe the bananas are, the batter may be slightly elastic and springy, so measure 100ml of cold water into a cup or jug and add a splash at a time, stirring well, to loosen it. When it pours thickly (rather than drops unceremoniously) from your spoon, you're ready to go.**

5 **Pour it into the cake tin and bake for 40 minutes, or until a knife or skewer inserted into the middle comes out clean. Transfer to a wire rack to cool. You can dust it with icing sugar, if you like, but I like to keep this one plain and fuss-free.**

CRUMBLY ALMONDY (ACCIDENTALLY GLUTEN-FREE) COOKIES (VE)

MAKES 10

100g ground almonds, plus extra for dusting

a pinch of chopped thyme leaves

a pinch of chopped lavender leaves

2 tbsp marmalade

5 tbsp butter substitute

Last night I really, really fancied cookies, in that way that sometimes the sweet tooth takes a hold. Usually it's late at night. Usually when I have resolved to be healthier, and better, and eat fewer baked goods in the smallest hours. Like on New Year's Day.

Succumbing, I pottered downstairs to the kitchen and rummaged in my flour bin (really, a bread bin full of various flours, with the ethos that if I want bread I will have to make it. Like a proper little bread martyr). The bread/flour bin turned out to be neither, as I had fed a few dozen people over the last few weeks of festivities, and somehow had managed to bake my way through my usual 3kg of plain flour kicking about the house. Instead, I had an array of what we might call 'experimental' flours, purchased in varying fits of panic over the last year or so, usually coinciding with some new health blogger or clean-eating trend, and then sitting, untouched, in the bottom of the flour bin. Until now.

I tipped out the bin. Quinoa flour. I definitely didn't buy that for myself. Brown rice flour – ah, that was for making pasta for my coeliac friend as a gift, that's legit, it can stay. Coconut flour – cheaper than coconut milk but can be blended into a rough approximation of it as required. Gram flour – useful for binding falafels and bhajis, and also makes an excellent fudge, allegedly, although I am yet to try it. And almond flour, simply a bag of ground almonds by another name. I will have cookies, I thought to myself, from one of these bags, I will have cookies.

I plumped for the almonds; crumbly, sweet, a relatively known entity, and accessible in a way that quinoa flour may not be in a bootstrap recipe, and these crumbly little morsels were born. I added thyme and lavender to mine – thyme as it was hanging about from Christmas, and lavender as it grows in my neighbour's garden, but neither are essential, so if you don't have them to hand, don't worry about buying them especially.

1 Preheat the oven to 180°C/350°F/gas 4 and lightly grease a baking sheet. Grab an egg cup, shot glass, espresso cup or small cookie cutter, and set to one side.

2 Tip the ground almonds into a bowl and add the thyme and lavender, if using.

3 In a separate small bowl, mash the marmalade and butter substitute together with a fork until well combined. Tip into the almonds and mix well until it forms a consistent dough.

4 Shake some ground almonds onto your worksurface and press or roll the dough out until around 1cm thick. Cut tiny cookie shapes – smaller than you think you need – and place on the baking sheet. Leave a large space in between each as they spread out when they warm through. Smoosh the dough back together and roll and repeat until there are no more cookies to be made.

5 Bake for 10 minutes. Remove from the oven and allow to cool for a further 10 minutes on the baking sheet, to harden, before trying to move them – they are deliciously crumbly, so they need some time to firm up before they are solid enough to cart about! Enjoy warm, and don't forget to send me photos if you make them – I love seeing you making my recipes!

DOUBLE-CHOCOLATE GUINNESS BROWNIES

MAKES 24 SMALL FAT
RICH BROWNIES

**250ml Guinness
(or other stout, if
your budget doesn't
stretch)**

200g dark chocolate

200g butter, diced

3 medium eggs

**300g granulated
sugar**

a pinch of salt

150g plain flour

100g milk chocolate

Firstly, for the budget-conscious among you raising eyebrows at the use of a bottle of the authentic black stuff in a batch of brownies, fear not, for this recipe makes 24 of the little tinkers and uses a little over half a can at that, so you could stretch to 40ish from a single can if you've a crowd to feed. If that doesn't satisfy you, well, most supermarkets sell an own-brand value range can of bitter at around £1 for 4 x 440ml cans.

But I created this on the eve of both my birthday and St Patrick's Day, so it had to be the real thing. I'm fussy about very little when it comes to ingredients in cooking, but Guinness makes my non-negotiable list, and I hope that you, dear readers, will note my half-Irish blood and birthday on St Paddy's Day and gently forgive me.

I first came across the idea of Guinness in cooking from the wonderful Nigella, in her book *Kitchen*, one of my go-to reads for comfort food and seductive words, to relax and unwind, to feel inspired, to find a moment of joy in food at the end of a long day. Her Guinness gingerbread with plums was the inspiration for my own Beery Berry Crumble in my first book, *A Girl Called Jack*, and both stand up to long cold days and a craving for a little comfort. As I mused aloud on Twitter that I was compiling my favourite Irish recipes for St Patrick's Day, several readers asked about a Guinness chocolate brownie. Intrigued, I experimented and explored, noted down several recipe variations, including my own brownie recipe scrawled into an old black notebook, and here we are: double-chocolate Guinness birthday brownies. I hope you love them as much as I do.

Recipe continues overleaf

1 Preheat the oven to 180°C/350°F/gas 4 and line a small roasting tray with baking parchment. If baking parchment isn't the kind of thing you have lying around, give the tray a good grease with oil to stop your brownies sticking.

2 Pour the Guinness into a small saucepan over low–medium heat. Perch a heatproof mixing bowl on the top – this will act as a bain-marie to simultaneously melt the butter and chocolate, and reduce the Guinness. Break up the dark chocolate only and pop it into the bowl with the butter, and heat for around 8 minutes to melt, stirring occasionally. Don't be tempted to crank up the heat, I did and my Guinness bubbled up and made a ghastly sticky mess all over my hob. Patience, it will all work out.

3 Meanwhile, beat together the eggs and sugar with the pinch of salt until well combined. Gradually add the flour, a quarter at a time, and beat it all in before adding the next batch. You can sift it for a smoother consistency, but a thorough beating with a wooden spoon will do the job just as well, with one less thing to wash up. When the chocolate and butter are melted and combined, gradually beat those into the mixture. Don't be tempted to splosh it all in at once, as searing hot chocolate and cold eggs has a lot of potential to go quite wrong … There's a reason why you don't generally see 'chocolate scrambled eggs' on restaurant menus!

4 When the melted chocolate and butter are combined with the eggs, flour and sugar, it's time to add the booze. It should have reduced by half (i.e. there should be 125ml there now, instead of 250ml, as half of it should have evaporated). If it hasn't, you can either carry on reducing it for a moment now it doesn't have a bowl of chocolate balancing on top, or just use 125ml of whatever quantity you have left – I can't imagine it will make a frightfully noticeable difference. Pour a little into the brownie mixture, mix well, and repeat until consistent. Pour the whole lot into your tray – it will be VERY runny. I had my doubts, slopping it in, that I was going to make anything that remotely resembled a brownie, so if you are pouring brownie soup into your tray with more than a touch of scepticism, you're doing it exactly right.

5 Break up your milk chocolate and poke the bits into the brownie soup at random intervals, and put the whole thing on the middle shelf of the oven. Close the door, and don't open it for 40 minutes, no matter how great it smells or how curious you are.

LEFTOVER STOLLEN (OR PANNETONE) ICE CREAM

SERVES 6–8

3 medium egg yolks (egg whites reserved for meringues – see Tip below – or egg-white omelettes)

100g granulated sugar

300ml double cream

100g stollen or pannetone

a pinch of salt

If you have some leftover pannetone or stollen kicking about from festivities and you're wondering what to do with it, of course you can slice it and freeze it, or fold it into a simple bread and butter pudding. But for a luxurious twist on a low budget I made a stollen ice cream.

This was a gift for a friend who I was seeing over the New Year, and a useful use-up for stray pots of cream lying around, too. It isn't vegan, as it's a rework of the semifreddo recipe in my cookbook *A Year In 120 Recipes*, so if anyone knows how to make a decent vegan semifreddo base, I'd be very interested to know!

Once mastered, this cheeky ice-cream recipe works with any stale cake and even bread crusts. What better destination for sad, tired birthday cake than to turn it into a huge bowl of ice cream?

1 Beat the yolks in a large mixing bowl with a whisk until creamy, and add the sugar. Beat again until well combined. If you have an electric whisk or mixer, it would come in very handy here, but if not, just give it some welly.

2 Add the cream and beat to form soft peaks. Again, this takes some effort, so put some music on and enlist other household members, if you have them, who can be won over with the promise of ice cream! When stiff and roughly doubled in size, set aside. Roughly chop the stollen or pannetone into small pieces. Dollop it into the bowl with the salt and gently fold it all through the ice-cream mixture, quickly but carefully, to avoid pushing the air out of it.

3 Pour the mixture into a freezerproof container. Cover with cling film and freeze for at least 4 hours.

4 Remove the ice cream from the freezer for at least 5 minutes before serving, to allow it to soften slightly. And enjoy!

TIP

● Don't throw away your egg whites when you separate the eggs. I generally make meringues with mine – 60g sugar to every egg white, beaten with a splash of vinegar until stiff, dolloped onto a baking tray, cooked at 130°C/250°F/gas ½ for 1 hour 15 minutes.

BROWN BREAD ICE CREAM

MAKES AROUND
8 PORTIONS

**100g wholemeal or
brown bread**

200ml whole milk

3 egg yolks

100g sugar

300ml double cream

a fistful of sultanas

FOR THE TOPPING

2 tsp breadcrumbs

1 tsp sugar

**a few pinches of
ground cinnamon**

I first discovered brown bread ice cream in an old copy of *Mrs Beeton's Everyday Cookery*, and as an avid maker of simple ice cream and brown bread, decided to combine my two recipes. You don't need an ice-cream maker for this one, I don't own one. If you have an electric whisk or cake mixer, it will come in handy, but you can make this without – you just need a little patience and a firm hand.

1 **Soak the bread in the milk and stand to one side for an hour or so.**

2 **Beat the egg yolks in a large mixing bowl until pale and fluffy. Add the sugar and beat well. Pour in the cream and whisk until the mixture has almost doubled in size. Run a finger through: it should feel airy, light and fluffy, and not fall off your finger. A common mistake is to beat too hard, knocking the air out of it as quickly as you beat it in – you want a firm and rhythmic hand, but not too much vigour. It should stand in soft peaks when you lift your whisk out. If you scrimp on this step, your ice cream will set rock hard, and while it won't be unpleasant, it will be that bit more difficult to eat.**

3 **Drain the milk from the brown bread, give it a gentle squeeze and tear it into small pieces. Fold it through the whipped cream mixture with the sultanas.**

4 **Pour it into a loaf tin or plastic container. Mix together the breadcrumbs, sugar and cinnamon and scatter over the top (if you forget this stage, you can do it just before serving). Cover the container with a lid or cling film to seal, and freeze for at least 4 hours.**

5 **Remove from the freezer 5 minutes before serving, to allow it to soften a little.**

PEAR AND ALMOND TART

SERVES 6

250g plain flour, plus extra for dusting

60g cold butter, diced

60g cold lard, diced

4 large ripe pears, skin left on and sliced finely, or peeled and diced

15g flaked almonds, roughly chopped, plus a few extra for the top

15g butter, melted

15g soft brown sugar

1 egg, beaten

ice cream, to serve (optional)

This simple fruit tart is based on one that I learned thirteen years ago in my high-school home economics classes – it's the first recipe I can remember being proud of. It didn't make it home, one of the pitfalls of having food class just before lunch break. The original recipe called for 'two tablespoons of dark rum', which my parents wouldn't let me take to school on the bus (I reckon they were worried I'd get tipsy and skip maths), so I did without it. I've made variations ever since, using whatever fruit is seasonal, cheap and available. The basic shortcrust pastry recipe has served me well over the years.

1 Preheat the oven to 180°C/350°F/gas 4. Lightly grease a baking sheet, or line it with baking parchment.

2 Put the flour in a large mixing bowl. Add the butter and lard, rubbing through with your fingers to a breadcrumb texture. Add some cold water, a tablespoon at a time, and bring the mixture together until you have a firm dough (you may need up to around 4½ tablespoons of water). Wrap the dough in cling film and chill for 15 minutes.

3 Put the pears in a bowl with the almonds, butter and sugar and mix well – you don't want a slushy mixture that will leak through your pastry, but you do want a pleasantly moist one.

4 Flour the work surface and roll the pastry to just shy of 1cm thick, then lay a large plate on top and cut around it. Transfer the pastry circle to the greased or lined baking sheet, then place the whole pear filling in the centre of the circle. Bring the pastry edges up and over the fruit, pleating it around, but leaving a gap in the centre to show the filling. Brush some egg over the pastry to glaze (use your fingers if you don't have a pastry brush). Bake in the centre of the oven for 1 hour until golden.

5 Allow to cool for a few minutes before serving with ice cream, if you like.

WHIRLY BUNS

MAKES A DOZEN
PLEASINGLY
ENORMOUS BUNS

750g plain flour, plus extra for dusting

500g natural yoghurt

100g sultanas or mixed dried fruit

up to 100ml warm water

13g dried active yeast

3 tbsp oil, plus extra for greasing

a pinch of salt

2 tsp ground cinnamon

2 tbsp sugar

These little weighty wistful whirls of whimsy came about entirely by accident. I was going to stay with friends in Manchester for the weekend, to all fling our small boys at one another for a raucous time, and I never like to accept hospitality empty handed. So I set about making a hulking great fruit bread, big enough to energise three grown men, three grown women and three small and boisterous boys. I mixed it, kneaded it, left it to rise … and promptly forgot all about it until I was halfway across the country. Bollocks. I came home to find it fermenting beautifully, tickling the top of the tea towel flung over the top of it. I gave it a ginger sniff, it smelled a lot like sourdough. Vaguely remembering a yoghurt-based bread I had made a few years ago, I figured it would be fine and whipped it into these whirly buns. J and A, here's what you could'a had … Sorry! (Pictured overleaf.)

1 Grab the largest mixing bowl you can find, and pour in the flour. These are dense, clunky buns, so there is no need to sift the flour. Just fling it in. Make a well (a sort of hole) in the centre as best you can, and slop the yoghurt into it, then shake in the fruit. Mix firmly to form a stiff dough. Some cheap yoghurts are quite sloppy, so this step should come easy, but if not, try using a knife instead of a spoon to mix it. The smooth flat edges of the knife act in a similar way to an industrial dough hook, and give a generally better result. Don't worry about this stage being too perfect, as there is more to come.

2 Take a mug and fill it with 100ml of warm water. It should be just warmish, too hot and you run the risk of killing off the poor yeast granules. Add the yeast and mix well, and leave to stand for a few minutes until it starts to bubble up – this is your yeast waking up from its slumber, and it never fails to amaze me! Tip it into the bigger bowl and add 1 tablespoon of oil and a pinch of salt, and mix until well combined.

3 Heavily flour your work surface and tip the dough onto it. Rub oil onto your hands to stop the dough from sticking to them, and knead it well for around 10 minutes. Push it away from you with your knuckles or palm, fold it back towards you, turn it a quarter-turn, and repeat. You'll find your own way of doing it, but it's therapeutic and fascinating as you feel the dough literally

take life beneath your hands. This is a heavy dough, so it will take some work; you can split it in half if you find it easier to work with smaller chunks.

4 When you're satisfied that you have pummelled it enough, put it to bed in the original mixing bowl, and cover with a clean tea towel or cling film. Pop it in a warm place for 3 hours (or longer – mine hung around for 3 days, remember).

5 When you're ready, take a small mug or bowl, and mix the cinnamon, sugar and remaining 2 tablespoons of oil together.

6 Tip the rested dough back onto a heavily floured surface. Give it a quick 30-second knead to push it back into shape but not so much as to knock the air out of it. Cut the dough into four equal-sized pieces, and set three to one side. Take one of the quarters and cut it into three. Roll one of the pieces (a twelfth of your original dough) into a long sausage shape about 5cm thick and as long as it gets. Take a rolling pin (or wine bottle) and roll the piece longways to flatten it. Using a pastry brush, teaspoon or your good trusty fingers, smear the sweet spicy oil across your dough. Then fold it in half horizontally to make a long, skinny piece of dough. It's less work than I'm making it sound, honest! And well worth it, trust me.

7 Brush the folded skinny piece of dough with the cinnamon oil again, then roll it into a whirl by taking one end and rolling it up to the other. Tuck the outside end under the bottom of the bun, and gently pat it on the head to press it all together. Lightly grease a large deep baking dish (you may need a couple depending on size) and pop your first bun into it and set aside. And repeat eleven times! Once you have the first one done, it's a breeze, I promise. A sweet, sticky, autumn-spiced breeze.

8 Now would be a good time to preheat the oven to 160°C/325°F/gas 3, and make sure the shelf is in the middle.

9 Pop the buns in the oven to bake for 1 hour. Allow them to cool before breaking one off for yourself, and digging in.

BEETROOT CHOCOLATE LOAF CAKE

SERVED 10

2–3 raw beetroots (the hard vegetable kind, not the pickled-in-vinegar kind), sliced

2 ripe bananas, peeled and broken into chunks

120ml oil

1 tsp bicarbonate of soda

200g coconut cream

275g plain flour

50g cocoa powder, or 100g dark chocolate, grated or finely chopped

100–200g sugar depending on taste (even at the 200g end, this is barely 2 tsp sugar each per slice)

Over one Christmas period I cooked four enormous meals in four different houses as four Christmas presents for friends and family. In mutual opinion and after a shitty bank fraud episode, it was the best Christmas present I could offer – swooping into someone else's kitchen and taking the stress out of catering for large groups of people, repurposing the leftovers into a pile of ready meals for the freezer, before packing my suitcase and moving on to the next house. It was a marvellous way to spend the week – I slept in six different beds in as many days and made a lot of new friends, drank a lot of wine, lost two knives along the way and had glorious fun. I made a host of new recipes as well – nothing gets my creative juices flowing like other people's sparse store-cupboards or a host of dietary requirements – and this was one of the winners. Faced with a stinking hangover from the night before's foray into homemade cranberry and orange vodka, a young guest with severe egg allergies and a limited supply of ingredients, I chanced upon a beetroot, threw it unpeeled into the blender, added it to a vegan chocolate cake recipe I had up my sleeve, and this was born. And oh, so sumptuous, so delicious, so gloriously purple, and the grateful grin from a little girl who can rarely eat cake at other people's houses made thinking through my hangover well worth it.

1 Preheat the oven to 180°C/350°F/gas 4.

2 Toss the beetroot into a blender with the bananas, oil, bicarb and coconut cream. Pulse to a vibrant pink paste, and scrape into a mixing bowl.

3 Add the flour, cocoa powder and sugar and mix well, adding a splash of water to loosen the mixture if required. Mix a bit more, and a bit more, to a glossy maroon batter. I fell in love with it at this point – the colour, the sweetness of the coconut milk and banana, the earthiness of the chocolate and raw beetroot. Having never made a beetroot cake before, I was pretty much blown away when I licked the spoon.

4 Lightly grease a 900g/2lb loaf tin and scrape in the batter mixture. Pop into the oven on the middle shelf for 45 minutes, or until a knife or skewer inserted into the middle comes out clean. And enjoy!

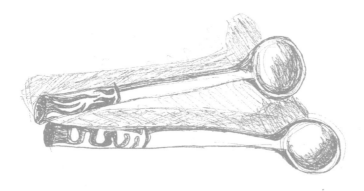

CHOUX PASTRY HEARTS

MAKES ABOUT 10

125g plain flour

1 tsp sugar

a pinch of salt

100g butter, diced

3 medium eggs, beaten

FOR THE FILLING

400ml double cream

2 tbsp icing sugar (or caster at a push)

1 vanilla pod, scraped, or a few drops of vanilla essence

FOR THE GANACHE

100g dark chocolate

a generous knob of butter

I first made choux pastry in the kitchen at Blackfoot, in Exmouth Market, ad hoc and accidentally. I did a few shifts to fill in some gaps in the rota and learn some new skills in a restaurant environment, rather than pottering around at home, and it was quite the baptism of fire. Recipes were scant lists of ingredients with scarce methods, several things were on the go at once, and almost everything was brand new to me, but I generally got my head down and worked it out, researching methods surreptitiously on Google in the corner, making copious notes, and studying recipe methods at the bar for hours after my shift. And then along came choux, that light and oh-so-crispy pastry, and I panicked. Tried to palm it off onto anyone else's prep list. 'I can't do this' – genuinely concerned for the first time since I'd donned a set of whites that there was something I was going to spectacularly fluff up. 'It's easy,' Rob, the head chef, soothed. 'Of course you can.' And I did. Because, as Rob said, it's easy.

These choux pastry hearts, incidentally, were inspired by a mooch through my CD collection, looking for something mellow and melodic to relax to a few weeks ago. I ended up with Corinne Bailey Rae's album, and Choux Pastry Heart, and here we are.

1 Sift the flour, sugar and salt into a bowl, one at a time. Some recipes sift the flour onto a sheet of baking parchment, but it's much of a muchness – I give them all a quick stir in a bowl and my choux is featherlight (a sentence I didn't ever imagine I'd say), so it's up to you.

2 Place 250ml cold water into a medium saucepan and add the diced butter. Place on medium heat and wait for the butter to melt. Once the butter has melted, increase the heat slightly and bring to the boil. Once boiling, immediately remove from the heat and add the flour mixture. Beat with a wooden spoon to form a smooth paste that will come away from the sides of the pan. Set to one side for a few minutes to cool.

Recipe continues overleaf

3 Preheat the oven to 220°C/450°F/gas 7. When the mixture has cooled to just warm to the touch, mix in the beaten eggs little by little. You probably won't need all the egg – stop adding it when the dough is glossy, soft and drops slowly from the wooden spoon. Either spoon the dough into a piping bag to pipe into heart shapes, or press gently into a heart-shaped cookie cutter, and repeat until all the dough is used up. Bake in the centre of the oven for 25 minutes, until risen and golden – DO NOT OPEN THE DOOR.

4 Meanwhile, pop barely 5cm water into a saucepan and balance a heatproof mixing bowl on top. Break the chocolate into chunks, and add to the bowl with the butter, then stir as they melt to combine the two and set aside to cool and thicken slightly.

5 In a separate bowl, beat the double cream with a little icing sugar and the scraped-out seeds of a vanilla pod or the vanilla essence, until the cream is stiff and doubled in size.

6 Remove from the oven and allow to cool for a minute before slicing in half. Place back into the oven for a further 5 minutes, cut-side up, to dry out.

7 To fill them, smear the cream filling generously onto the bottom half of your heart, and sandwich back together. Spoon on your chocolate ganache, or draw chocolate heart shapes onto the choux buns and leave to set. And voilà – stored in an airtight container, they'll last for 3 days in the fridge. Mine didn't . . .

TIPS

● You need a piping bag and nozzle or a heart-shaped cookie cutter for this. I opted for the cutter, because I can be fairly indelicate with a piping bag.

● It is best to store the buns before they are filled as the filling can make them soggy. When you want to serve, place them in an oven preheated to 200°C/400°F/gas 6 to crisp up for 5 minutes, then fill.

RHUBARB AND CUSTARD RICE PUDDING

SERVES 4

200g rhubarb stalks, cut into bite-sized chunks

50g sugar

150g long grain rice, rinsed

600ml whole milk

385g shop-bought custard

There is nothing as comforting as rhubarb and custard to see you through the last of the winter's chill. Traditional rice pudding is baked in the oven, but I never heat up the whole oven for something I can do just as well on the hob. (Pictured overleaf.)

1 Pop the rhubarb chunks in a small saucepan and cover with water. Add the sugar, bring to the boil over high heat, then lower the heat and simmer for 5 minutes. Remove the rhubarb with a slotted spoon and reserve on a plate to serve on top of the pudding.

2 Add the rice to the rhubarb poaching water with the milk and bring back to the boil before reducing the heat and simmering for 20 minutes, or until soft, sticky and creamy.

3 Stir in the custard before serving, and top with the chunks of rhubarb.

TIP

● If you're cooking something else in the oven at around 180°C/350°F/gas 4, put all the ingredients for the custard rice pudding in a lidded casserole dish for half an hour or so on the bottom shelf.

TAHINI AND ORANGE PEEL SEMIFREDDO

1 large orange

4 large eggs

200g caster sugar

a pinch of salt

100g tahini paste

300ml double cream

I first made a version of this for the *Cook For Syria* cookbook, fundraising for victims of the ongoing war in Syria, yet that one was a tahini and rosewater semifreddo with a pistachio crumb. I have toned it down a little here, well aware that in my most 'bootstrap' days, a packet of pistachios would have cost me half of my weekly budget, and so the idea of including them here seems louche and inappropriate. Tahini can be found very cheaply in ethnic grocery stores and the world food aisle of supermarkets, but in its absence, peanut butter is a fine substitute.

1 Grate the zest from the outside of the orange with a sharp knife, microplane or grater. Set to one side – you'll be needing this later.

2 Next, line a 900g/2lb loaf tin or other small receptacle with two layers of cling film, using your fingers to push it into the corners, with a few centimetres spare all round – this is to make the semifreddo easy to remove later. If you don't have any cling film, you can skip this step, but it can get a little messy.

3 Separate the eggs and refrigerate the whites to use for something else – meringues, cake, an egg white omelette. Pop the yolks into a large mixing bowl and pour in the sugar, add two-thirds of the zest and the salt and tahini, and beat together until the yolks are white and fluffy, and the mixture has doubled in size.

4 Add the cream, squeeze in the juice from the orange, and beat well until it forms stiff peaks – I used to have to make this with a friend on hand to take turns at beating it, but I seem to be able to do it all by myself these days! If you have an electric whisk or stand mixer loitering around, now would be a great time to get it out, but if not it's a labour of love – put some loud music on and get a rhythm going, and it will be done before you know it.

5 When the cream is light and fluffy and forms soft peaks – slowly drops off an overturned spoon or fingers – you're good to go. Pop the remaining zest into the bottom of the loaf tin and give it a shake to disperse it along the bottom – when turned out, it will sit pretty on the top. Get as arty as you like with it, but I just like it flung all over.

6 Carefully spoon the cream mixture into the loaf tin and give it a gentle shake to get it into all the corners, then smooth the top. Carefully fold the cling film over the top, and pop in the freezer for at least 4 hours to set. Remove and leave to soften before serving.

PERFECT CHOCOLATE CHIP COOKIES

MAKES 24

60g salted butter, diced

150g granulated sugar

60ml sunflower oil

1 medium egg

1 tsp bicarbonate of soda

240g plain flour

35g dark chocolate, chopped into chips,

When I devised this recipe I was a bit miserable, the gas meter was running out, my tiny flat was cold and I was generally feeling a little grouchy and blue. Usual distractions didn't apply – I didn't own a television and nor did I have broadband to distract myself from the occasional bout of gloom.

So, cookies. I put a rallying cry on Twitter, as the wonderful people who follow me are often so very generous at sharing their favourite recipes and ideas when I feel in need of inspiration. My cookie-need was met by these gorgeous beauties, from Felicity Cloake's 'How To Cook The Perfect ...' column in the *Guardian*. I tweaked her recipe a bit, as I didn't have the right sugar in, I was light on chocolate, and there was no way I was waiting 12–24 hours for the dough to chill, and since Sainsbury's seem to have discontinued their Basics butter there's no way I'm slinging half a block of the alternative into a batch of cookies, so I replaced half the butter with oil. And here's my midnight delight.

1 Preheat the oven to 180°C/350°F/gas 4 and lightly grease a baking tray. Let the butter come to room temperature, or if you're in a hurry for baked goods, as I was, pop it into a microwave-safe bowl and ping for 10 seconds to cheat it. No longer, please, as the butter starts to separate and for some reason this massively mucks up your baking, cos ... science.

2 Cream the butter and sugar together with a fork or wooden spoon and some good hard smooshing and stirring. This is therapeutic. I often find if I am desperate for baked goods in the middle of the night, I have some things to work through, and this step is very useful for that.

3 Add the oil and the egg and mix thoroughly. Now add the bicarb and the flour, and mix well to form a dough. Fold through the chocolate chips.

4 Add golf-ball-sized pieces of dough to the greased baking tray. Flatten them slightly with the prongs of a fork, and place very far apart as they will flatten and spread as they cook. I only cooked a third of the mixture, because I don't trust myself with twenty-four cookies, and will freeze the rest for future midnight-cookie-needs or Christmas presents.

5 Bake in the centre of the oven for 12 minutes or until the edges are golden. Remove from the oven and allow to cool for a few minutes before moving – they will crumble if you move them too soon! Remove when ready and pile on a plate to continue cooling, or a wire rack if you have one (I don't, so fold a clean tea towel into four and place on a plate, and pile the cookies onto that to absorb any excess moisture).

6 Devour, and store any left (ha!) when completely cooled, in an airtight container. Don't store them hot, they will create a nice sweaty wet environment and go mouldy and nasty and … science. Again.

TIPS

• I use ordinary granulated sugar in my cookies, Felicity recommends half granulated and half soft brown, but I didn't have any in. For what it's worth, I only keep granulated sugar in the house, and if a recipe calls for 'caster', and I think it genuinely needs it, like a cake or something, I blitz the granulated stuff in the blender to make it finer. It's always worked for me. Again, science.

• If you're the kind of person who buys those large bags of festive nuts at Christmas and is still looking at them in a few months' time, this recipe is a great place to fling them. Crack them, chop them and make them into cookies.

THANKS

This is an updated, full-colour version of the crowd-funded, limited edition *Cooking on a Bootstrap* published in 2017.

The illustrations are by Birdy Rose, John Bulley, Bonnie Blueman and Hattie: all well-loved local artists from Southend-on-Sea, Essex. (And a few by me, not an artist, just a doodler).

With thanks to Carole, Martha and Hockley at Bluebird. To Rosemary, Aoife and Natalia for tough love and tougher deadlines. Thanks to Mike for his creative and beautiful photography. Thanks Mum and Dad for kicking my ass to the end of this; Nan for motivational raised eyebrows about 'quite' how long it was taking; and Cat, Phil, Imogen and Emily for being willing guinea pigs as well as dear friends. Georgi and Caz for your endless support and motivation; Vix for hours of hard slog and harder spirits; and with all my love, and thank you for rebuilding me, sustaining me, and refusing to take my starving artist diva crap, Louisa, I don't know why you put up with me, but the pancakes are all yours.

INDEX

Vegan recipes are highlighted in blue type (although many other recipes in the book can be easily adapted to suit vegan diets)

First published 2018 by Bluebird
an imprint of Pan Macmillan

20 New Wharf Road, London N1 9RR
Associated companies throughout the world www.panmacmillan.com

ISBN 978-1-5098-3111-1

9 8 7 6 5 4 3 2 1

A CIP catalogue record for this book is available from the British Library.

Printed and bound in China.

Publisher Carole Tonkinson

Senior Editor Martha Burley

Assistant Editor Hockley Raven Spare

Senior Production Controller Ena Matagic

Art Direction & Design Andrew Barron / Thextension

Prop & Food Styling Kate Wesson

Visit www.panmacmillan.com to read more about all our books and to buy them. You will also find features, author interviews and news of any author events, and you can sign up for e-newsletters so that you're always first to hear about our new releases.